Praise for *The Fragility of Language and the Encounter with God*

"In this meditation on the relationship between God and human language, Florian Klug addresses the fundamental question of theology: What does it mean for human beings to speak of God? Weaving together biblical testimony and Lacanian psychoanalysis, continental thought and conciliar documents, this book charts a promising course for Catholic theology by reimagining authority, not as an assertion of sovereign domination, but as an encounter and an opening to freedom."

—Adam Kotsko, author of *Neoliberalism's Demons*

"This is a deeply innovative and intelligent book. Klug works dynamically in the borderlands between theology, continental philosophy, and psychoanalytic thought, demonstrating the value of numerous figures in the latter two traditions for pursing major questions about the nature of Christian faith, truth, and divine revelation. Klug is particularly interested in the question of humanity's authority over God: the possibility of naming and speaking about the divine. Having defined humans as hermeneutical beings, their worlds limited by their language, Klug engages Jacques Lacan and Slavoj Žižek to develop an account of encounter with God as radical intrusion or imposition from the outside. The outcome of this study is a stimulating interpretation of doctrine in the Catholic tradition as proclamations of hope and anticipation—attempts to live in the gulf between human historicity and the intrusion of God into the world."

—Ruth Jackson Ravenscroft, fellow in theology and philosophy of religion at Sidney Sussex College, University of Cambridge

"*The Fragility of Language and the Encounter with God* is an excellent contribution to the theology of God and language. It is a wide-ranging, interdisciplinary treatment, engaging with Scripture, postmodern philosophy, and philosophical theology, which offers a challenging and fundamental contribution to current debates on church doctrine and authority."

—Stephan Van Erp, professor of fundamental theology, KU Leuven

"This is an important book because it reminds women and men of today that the Christian God is a God of history. This has enormous consequences in order to understand the importance of language and ritual for religion and faith, in our age of god-like, all-powerful algorithms and big data."

—Massimo Faggioli, professor of theology and religious studies, Villanova University, and author of *The Liminal Papacy of Pope Francis: Moving Toward Global Catholicity* (2020) and *Joe Biden and Catholicism in the United States* (2021)

"*The Fragility of Language and the Encounter with God* is a book for which many of us have been waiting, a book that sets a path forward for theologians and philosophers of religion who wish to bring the contributions of phenomenology, deconstruction, philosophy of language, and psychoanalysis to bear on one of the most persistent and difficult issues in theology: the nature of the linguistic mediation of the relationship between God and human beings. With wisdom, discernment, and a good deal of savvy, Florian Klug models not only a deep and abiding commitment to a *fides quaerens intellectum*, but also the kind of intellectual charity, conceptual breadth, and genuine insight that characterize modern systematic theology at its best."

—Jay Martin, assistant teaching professor, University of Notre Dame

"*The Fragility of Language and the Encounter with God* offers a profound theological reflection on the nature of and the constraints placed on our ability to speak of God. This creative study persuasively underscores doctrine's role within the church's life as a response to, and as mediating an encounter with, the God revealed by Jesus Christ who remains *semper maior*. Led by Klug to the limits of speech, one may discover oneself drawn by the Spirit into the *mysterium* of Christ to which the church's doctrines point."

—Ryan G. Duns, SJ, assistant professor of theology, Marquette University, author of *Spiritual Exercises for a Secular Age: Desmond and the Quest for God*

THE FRAGILITY OF LANGUAGE AND THE ENCOUNTER WITH GOD

THE FRAGILITY OF LANGUAGE AND THE ENCOUNTER WITH GOD

On the Contingency and Legitimacy of Doctrine

Florian Klug
Foreword by Marcus Pound

Translated by
Barbara Stone

FORTRESS PRESS
MINNEAPOLIS

THE FRAGILITY OF LANGUAGE AND THE ENCOUNTER WITH GOD
On the Contingency and Legitimacy of Doctrine

Translated by Barbara Stone from the German Sprache, Geist und Dogma: Über den Einbruch Gottes in die Wirklichkeit des Menschen und dessen sprachliche Aufarbeitung (Ferdinand Schöningh, 2016).

Cover image: "The Crucifixion" by Jean Francois Portaels (1886). Sedmak/iStock
Cover design: Brice Hemmer

Print ISBN: 978-1-5064-7368-0
eBook ISBN: 978-1-5064-7369-7

Contents

Foreword

by
Marcus Pound

Make no mistake about it, this book is a comic book—comic in the sense that its affirmation of the truth and validity of doctrine outstrips postmodern skepticism, even as it cedes the ground to postfoundational truth; comic in its affirmation of gospel revelation, even as the text appears to crumble under the weight of successive interpretation; and comic in the sense that it marks a decisive moment in the theological reception of Jacques Lacan, one marked not by the tragedy of an ever-receding and ungraspable truth but by the laughter that accompanies a step in the dance through which doctrine is weaved and affirmed in a moment of shared ecclesial joy.

Lacan famously declared in his playful inversion of Descartes, "I am thinking where I am not, therefore I am where I am not thinking," which was his way of framing the question of authority once the confidence of the ego was shaken:[1] What authority do we have over ourselves in our capacity as speaking beings? Moreover, What authority do we have to speak of God?

For Lacan, the paradox of authority was the paradox of language: we identify ourselves through language but only at the expense of losing ourselves in it as objects. The result? Language fails to say it all, and hence truth is always half-said in a way that gives rise to unconscious desire.

As Klug points out, Lacan furnishes us with a set of conceptual tools by which to approach the paradox of a community built on the authority of a god who only speaks his half name—the paradox of a god who is closer to us than we are to ourselves in a way that speaks to the Real of the human desire.

But why should this mark a comic turn in the theological reception of Lacan? Lacan initially arrived in the Anglophone world mediated through literary theory, traveling via the intellectual currents of North America in the 1970s to revive the

1. Jacques Lacan, *Écrits: The First Complete Edition in English*, trans. Bruce Fink, in collaboration with Héloïse Fink and Russell Grigg (New York: W. W. Norton, 2006), 430.

ailing humanities under the weight of "new criticism." More often than not, he was lumped together with Jacques Derrida and Roland Barthes under various rubrics from "structuralist" to "postmodern" in ways that helped, at the very least, make sense of the linguistic turn within French intellectual thought.

The orientation of his reception was distinctly Heideggerian. While Derrida translated the *Destruktion* of Being into the deconstruction of the metaphysics of a text, Lacan was busy unpicking the metaphysics of the Freudian ego as understood within the currents of American ego psychology. Where Heidegger entertained language as the "house of being," Lacan took language as the house of the unconscious: the unconscious is structured like a language.

However, given his perceived proximity to Derrida, and the sense that postmodernism was to nihilism what Marxism was to atheism, the import of Lacan's work was often presented and defended in terms of the primary of the ethical à la Levinas—that is, the postmodern injunction against idolatry. Understood this way, the import of Lacanian analysis was not to provoke any triumph of self-awareness; rather, it was to uncover the unconscious structures that give rise to our neuroses in a process of constant decentering, during which the subject delves into the loss of her own mastery.

Translated theologically? Lacan reminds us that all theological discourse is a form of speech, and it therefore speaks of a lack; like the analyst, the aim should be to highlight the way theology was falsely unified (the ego) through institutional forms when desire (i.e., lack) was lost sight of. By ceding mastery, theology could become less concerned with defending doctrine and become instead an ethical venture in freedom: letting things be in their "Otherness."

Arguably, however, such an approach quickly yields, on the one hand, a theology drained of all authority or institutional moorings and, on the other hand, a postmodern apologetic for the theological significance of the via negativa. From the standpoint of Lacan, these are merely two variations of the theological imaginary: either the isolation of the solitary and marginal wanderer without context or community or those who would all the while secretly affirm the absent Master, two versions of a theology stuck within the register of the tragic, condemned to the fate of Sisyphus by the inevitable promise and loss that language bares.

Slavoj Žižek's project to reread German idealism on the basis of Lacan—repeating Hegel in the manner that Lacan repeated Freud—helped shift the reception of Lacan in two important ways, which are reflected in this work. First, he provides a comic reading of Lacan: rather than being resigned to the impossibility of speaking the truth directly (Kantian epistemology), the truth happens precisely as the impossible encounter (Hegelian dialectics). Second, in a manner that recalls the Kierkegaardian leap of faith, Žižek underlines the eventful significance of the impossible encounter as giving rise to the truth event: an occurrence that intrudes from the outside and invalidates the existing order at the point one not only recognizes it as the truth but, in a moment of decisiveness, commits in favor of this truth.

For Klug, Christ is that event, the "friendly" trauma, and the question turns more specifically on the subsequent codification of Christ's truth in successive waves of councils and doctrine. Here, the work takes on a distinctly Catholic approach that indirectly recalls Louis-Marie Chauvet's imposing work *Symbol and Sacrament*.

Chauvet explored the implications of Lacan's linguistic model in his development of a "foundational theology of sacramentality."[2] At the heart of his work was a rejection of any appeal to the objective efficacy of the sign given in neoscholastic treatments of the sacraments. This, he argued, served primarily to reinforce the centrality of a hierarchical church and situate power in the hands of the priest at the expense of the laity by fetishizing God's presence into the locality of the Eucharist object. Drawing on Lacan's articulation of the symbolic, he made the case that there are no exemptions from the human conditions of desire, language, embodiment, and history and that theologically speaking, the entire horizon of Christian faith is always already inscribed in the order of the sacramental.

What Klug presents here amounts to a "foundational theology of doctrine" that, like Chauvet, argues that human beings do not simply possess and use language as a tool but are actually born into an inherited language, a culture, a symbolic world of meaning. Human beings only ever come to know the "world" and to become relational subjects within it through the symbolic mediation of communication.

And where Chauvet argues that we should conceive the sacraments not as intermediaries between God and humankind but as "expressive" mediations of the church and the believer in the mode of and within language, Klug argues that doctrines also are expressive mediations of the church and believer in the mode

2. Louis-Marie Chauvet, *Symbol and Sacrament: A Sacramental Reinterpretation of Christian Existence*, trans. Patrick Madigan, SJ, and Madeleine Beaumont (Collegeville, MN: Liturgical, 1995), 1.

of language in a way that gives renewed sense to the pneumatological meaning of *sensus fidelium*: doctrines are statements of hope.

And finally, like Chauvet, the wager of this piece is whether we can situate the problematic of language, God, and doctrine in the context of Heidegger's critique of metaphysics, advanced through Lacan. Such a gesture requires, on the one hand, resisting the desire to "recover" God's revelation in the manner of platonic recollection, and on the other hand, neither should it betray God's most essential aspect. Klug manages both in a way that recalls something of the comic's ability to hold in tension two opposing frames of reference. Klug masterfully manages those tensions within the frame of speech and revelation to provide an innovative approach to understanding not simply the conditions that give rise to doctrine but, crucially, our role in that process.

Preface to the English Edition

> I am writing about God; I expect few readers and only await agreement from some of them.
>
> —Diderot, *Pensées philosophiques*

Even though it is a precarious undertaking, the preoccupation with God is a theologian's daily bread. Additionally, if the theologian is questioning man's view of reality from the perspective of God's intervention, it can lead to a critical examination of his own reality because of his increasing awareness of its fragility. Becoming aware of my own precarious state, I want to express words of thanks to those persons who have offered me assistance, support, and encouragement during the composition of this work and the subsequent adventure of translation.

First and foremost, I thank Otmar Meuffels for encouraging me to explore an unusual approach to the doctrine of the Catholic Church. He has always made himself available to me at critical junctures. I am grateful to know Jürgen Bründl, for he provided guidance and discussed numerous ideas early on.

Motivation and encouragement for this translation came from many people, and I thank them all for their advice. I owe special thanks to my wife, Janina Klug, because her words always revived my own enthusiasm. I sincerely express my thanks to Paul D. Murray and the staff of the Center for Catholic Studies at Durham University for introducing me into English-speaking academia. Especially, I express my gratitude to Marcus Pound for being a remarkable friend and a steady counsel over the last years. I also want to say thanks to Adam Kotsko for introducing me to outstanding scholars and encouraging me to think outside the box. Particularly, I want to say thanks to Barbara Stone, who did an incredible job in translating this work. Her devotion to the task and her eye for details impressed me time and again, and her questions during the process of translation have helped give more transparency to the text. Because "no man is an island," it would be fatal in a theological inquiry to simply reiterate one's own views. One would end up with the same knowledge that one had at the start. I, therefore, want to once again express my sincerest gratefulness to those mentioned above.

Florian Klug
Bayreuth, March 2021

Translator's Note

I offer a few notes regarding decisions I have made in translating this text into English. Given the variety of sources used in this book, I have often needed to treat texts in different ways. My primary aim in this translation has been to use texts in English that are readily accessible to an English reader.

For the translation of passages from Vatican I and Vatican II, see the note at the beginning of the bibliography.

Bibliographic references in English indicate works originally written in English or previously published English translations of non-English texts; bibliographic references in German or other non-English languages indicate works that have not been translated into English or, in a very few cases, works that have been translated but are difficult to access in the United States. Translations of quotations taken from bibliographic references in German are my own. Whenever page references are given in nonnumerical order, the listing goes from the most relevant and important to those of lesser importance.

The English and German uses of pronouns and gendered language are very different; this presents an enormous challenge to contemporary translators, especially when working with theological texts treating biblical topics. I have sought to offer a readable text that avoids awkward wordings and pronoun usage that can result from "modernized" discussions/interpretations of theological texts. As in the original sources, I have used male pronouns in referring to God and the Holy Spirit, and I have used man/men, humans/humanity, or male pronouns when referring to the Israelites and other peoples. This decision does not imply a critique of feminism or of more contemporary English language usage; it is a straightforward recognition of the characteristics of the German language and biblical sources.

I have made some choices about the use of a few specific German terms. I note the following:

Because this book implicitly relies in large part on Heideggerian philosophy, wherever the German text uses the word *Sein* (Being) or compound words derived from *Sein*, I have given the original German term in parentheses following my English rendering.

I have translated the German word *Dogma* and other words derived from it as "doctrine" or "doctrinal" to avoid the negative connotations of the English words *dogma* and *dogmatic*. In this context, the word *dogma* refers to the field of study of Catholic doctrine and doctrinal history.

I thank Florian Klug for his openness and cooperation throughout the entire process. It has been a joy to work with him. He has been patient, witty, and extraordinarily helpful in our discussions of matters both large and small, from the details and complexities of Catholic doctrine to the minutiae of editorial decisions. I thank the staff of Styberg Library on the Northwestern University campus for being so welcoming and supportive of my work and use of their collection. I especially thank Harold Stone, professor of European history at the Shimer School of North Central College, for his advice, historical knowledge, and editorial skills. His assistance has supported and sustained me throughout this project.

Barbara S. Stone

October 2019

Introduction

The Primary Epistemological Question

This work investigates the question of man's authority over God: To what extent is man granted access to the Judeo-Christian God by knowing his name and being able to use it? Is man granted power over the Divine Being through his ability to formulate declarative statements—statements that stand out because they are about the Divine Being? Are human statements, by definition, true and correct if their contents are about God, the Creator of Being (Sein) and the world—about the God whom Christians believe revealed himself to them through Jesus Christ (*Dei verbum* [DV] 2, 972) and whom the Gospel according to John says nothing less than this: he is "the way, and the truth, and the life" (John 14:6)? Aren't these sentences, by necessity, true and correct because man can confer upon them, from within, a divine quality through God's name? Or to the contrary, does man find himself in a precarious situation because he himself has no power over language and is therefore simultaneously at risk of becoming a heretic?

Man's ability to even speak about God and make statements about him is not self-evident; it is based on God's initial move toward man. God turns toward man, reveals himself to man, and tells him his name so that man will have access to God (Exod 3:14). The fact that a person can say "God" (in the Christian sense) or does not enunciate the Tetragrammaton out of reverence and respect for God does not result from a deduction or a syllogism but is opened in God's devotion to man. It begins with God's turning toward man; God reveals himself and his identity to man.

This is the beginning of the investigation: What power was granted to man when God told him his name? Does man thereby gain the authority to make definitive statements because he speaks about the Absolute that has turned toward him?

More precisely, this investigation pursues the subject of doctrine because a Christian's, and especially a Catholic's, understanding of truth is particularly important. Because the term *dogmatic* connotes, in everyday German language usage, a lack of reflection, an obstinance, and an unwillingness to reconsider one's position, this investigation offers a special opportunity to ask what authority the church's magisterium as the office of doctrine has—that is, has been granted—in regard to truth and validity in matters of professions of faith.

1

Man and Language

Man as a Speaking Being

Since antiquity, those who have observed man, and seek to define the qualities that are unique to him and differentiate him from other living creatures—especially from other animals—have focused on the rational language of Logos that has been granted to man. This places him above all animals.[1] For man, language is the means of communication par excellence; through language, man can enter into a mediating and a mediated relationship with a counterpart, with an Other. Just as a speaking being is in a relationship with a recipient, the relationship between a speaking being and language likewise consists of an irrevocable alterity. Language is acquired from the external world, through experience; in the communicative process, one's focus shifts from one's own position toward that of the interlocutor. Language always remains something external to man; it can't be incorporated into one's own self—that is, into one's own horizon—in such a way that one would have real authority over it. The externality, the inaccessibility, and the alterity of language are essential elements of human speech.

If language lacked these characteristics, it would be in danger of losing its dynamism, its ability to develop, and its vitality; it would tend toward stasis. If that were to happen, there would no longer be understanding, but only direct knowledge. Therefore, according to Martin Heidegger, speaking and expressing are not the primary starting points for man's ability to speak; man's ability to listen is prior to even having words: "Listening to . . . is the existential being-open of Dasein as being-with for the other. Listening even constitutes the primary and authentic

1. See Aristotle, *Politics*, in *The Complete Works of Aristotle: The Revised Oxford Translation*, ed. Jonathan Barnes, vol. 2 (Princeton, NJ: Princeton University Press, 1984): "Man is the only animal who has the gift of speech" (1988 [1253a]).

openness of Dasein for its ownmost possibility of being, as in hearing the voice of the friend whom every Dasein carries with it."[2]

In addition, one should note a special characteristic of human speech that is closely associated with the etymological relationship between λόγος and logic: human speech and human thought can't, and mustn't, be strictly separated from one another. Moreover, according to Hans-Georg Gadamer, there is an essential connection between thought and speech that keeps them closely intertwined with each other: "*Rather, language is the universal medium in which understanding occurs. Understanding occurs in interpreting*. . . . All understanding is interpretation, and all interpretation takes place in the medium of a language that allows the object to come into words and yet is at the same time the interpreter's own language."[3]

It must be noted that human language is not an instrument,[4] an object that man can use independent of thought; if that were the case, language would only emerge secondarily—that is, be an additional factor that helps man articulate his thoughts aloud and communicate them to fellow human beings. Man is a historical being embedded in historical structures that he can certainly recognize but can't overcome. This temporary horizon has a special quality: the time-bound nature of linguistic access to the world is expressed anew in each spoken word. Following Gadamer, one can say that man, due to his own historicity, is always subject to a linguistic prejudgment that is open to being revised or corrected.[5] An "a priori" prior to this prejudgment can't exist because man is dependent on experiences that come to him from the outside. Through experience, man acquires language, knowledge, and a horizon as a structurally necessary prejudgment; it is precisely through this same experience of an intrusion from the external world that a prejudgment, if man is open to it, will be revised or corrected.[6]

2. Martin Heidegger, *Being and Time*, trans. Joan Stambaugh, rev. Dennis J. Schmidt (Albany: State University of New York Press, 2010), 158.
3. Hans-Georg Gadamer, *Truth and Method*, rev. and trans. Joel Weinsheimer and Donald G. Marshall, 2nd ed. (London: Continuum, 2006), 390.
4. The idea of treating language as an instrument first explicitly appears in Plato, *Cratylus*, in *The Collected Dialogues of Plato*, ed. Edith Hamilton and Huntington Cairns (Princeton, NJ: Princeton University Press, 1987), 426 (388a–b).
5. See Gadamer, *Truth and Method*, 269–70, 303, 390. Thus Gadamer pleads for the rehabilitation of the concept of a prejudgment as a necessary premise in order to be able to express the historically conditioned perspective of each person in a way that can be understood. See also Gadamer, 296–97.
6. See Gadamer, 350–51.

Man can't take an objective position toward language—that is, treat it as a concrete object or an instrument. Walter Kasper, following Heidegger and his student Gadamer, takes the view that man depends on language in order to even have access to hearing the truth. However, the same words can't directly present the truth to man because they are independent of man; they are integrated in a dialectic movement that makes the truth accessible or inaccessible.[7] Man is dependent on language in order to be able to think. He can't violently reject this dependence and become his own master of language because this would place him outside the world and historicity. In other words, a human being who frees language from these conditions and then places himself in an absolute position over language is no longer a human being.[8] Man's world of understanding is a world of language; his horizon is located in this world and can be expanded. Man experiences the world through language, but language is not a direct reproduction of reality; it gives humans the possibility of having access to reality.[9] Man gains perspective through language. It is finite and limited, just as Wittgenstein's perspective toward the world through language claims, "*The limits of my language* mean the limits of my world."[10]

Limitations and Possibilities of Human Speech

Even though man's authority over language is limited, and he can never really master it, language opens up possibilities for him that can only exist through language and can never exist beyond it. Language gives man the possibility of not only being able to act in a practical way; through speech itself, via so-called performative statements, man is able to produce objective facts about reality.[11]

As already mentioned, language is, first and foremost, an event between people in which a speaking being enters into a relationship with an Other. John R. Searle,

7. See Walter Kasper, *Dogma unter dem Wort Gottes* (Mainz, Germany: Matthias-Grünewald-Verlag, 1965), 61–65.
8. What this shows, in regard to access to language, is equally valid for man's knowledge of himself: therefore, Slavoj Žižek, following Kant, can also say, "This in-between—neither phenomenal nor noumenal, but the gap which separates the two and, in a way, precedes them—'is' the subject." Slavoj Žižek, *The Ticklish Subject: The Absent Centre of Political Ontology* (London: Verso, 2000), 25.
9. See Gadamer, *Truth and Method*, 443–44.
10. Ludwig Wittgenstein, *Tractatus Logico-Philosophicus*, trans. D. F. Pears and B. F. McGuiness, with an introduction by Bertrand Russell (London: Routledge, 1981), 56 (5.6).
11. See John Langshaw Austin, *How to Do Things with Words: The William James Lectures Delivered at Harvard University in 1955* (Cambridge, MA: Harvard University Press, 1962), 94–107.

in his work on the construction of human institutions through human speech acts, declares that language is primarily a functional instrument that is available to humans and makes it possible for them to live in a communicative community with one another.[12] Because language is not a direct reproduction of external reality, and it can't be (as a medium for communication, language has a mediating position and therefore occupies the middle between a thing and its meaning), it can lead to differences—that is, disagreements between signification (the sign—the signifier—and the signified).[13] The relationship between the signifier and the signified is not natural and directly given: "The link between signal and signification is arbitrary. Since we are treating a sign as the combination in which a signal is associated with a signification, we can express this more simply as: *the linguistic sign is arbitrary*."[14]

Language and its linguistic signs are not an identical reproduction of reality; to the contrary, they are separated by a chasm that humans can't overcome through logical-rational means. Man can recognize this gap between the signifier and the signified and problematize it, as Jacques Derrida and others do with the neologism *différance*.[15] One finds here the essential mystery of human language; due to the contingency of its function as a sign, it opens up possibilities of naming and signifying, but it also simultaneously, in turn, closes and even denies man the possibility of mastering it. Language can be understood as a wound or as something in a state of limbo.[16] Even thematicizing and articulating this mystery doesn't reveal it, nor does this lead it to an enlightened position; rather, it focuses one's gaze onto the mystery so that man, despite all his difficulties and efforts to analyze language, has no choice but to accept his inability to master language and its state of limbo. Man can only respond to the question of the essence of language by a paradoxical nonresponse.[17]

12. See John R. Searle, *Making the Social World: The Structure of Human Civilization* (Oxford: Oxford University Press, 2010), 71.
13. See Ferdinand de Saussure, *Course in General Linguistics*, ed. Charles Bally and Albert Sechehaye, trans. Roy Harris (Chicago: Open Court, 2003), 66–69. See also Gerhard Schönrich, "Semiotik," in *Enzyklopädie Philosophie*, vol. 2, O–Z (Hamburg, Germany: Meiner, 1999), 1463–64.
14. Saussure, *Course in General Linguistics*, 67.
15. See Jacques Derrida, "Différance," in *Margins of Philosophy*, trans. Alan Bass (Chicago: University of Chicago Press, 1982), 15–17.
16. See Jacques Derrida, *On the Name*, ed. Thomas Dutoit, trans. David Wood, John P. Leavey Jr., and Ian McLeod (Stanford, CA: Stanford University Press, 1995), 27-28.
17. See Derrida, 19–21.

The problem that a linguistic sign doesn't directly reproduce the signified object phonetically but only references and names it in a declarative statement isn't made any easier if one places various signs in relation to one another and if one connects them functionally through grammatical structures and forms a statement out of all of them. Nevertheless, as precarious as this starting point is for man's attempts to solve this problem, this opens up the possibility for man, on a practical level, to not only take an individual position but enter into a communicative community with another person in which he is totally reliant on himself as a creature that is a speaking being. In speech, man puts himself at risk as an individual by marking his statements with an I and identifying them as his own individual perspective.[18]

A speaking being finds himself in a dialectical situation; he doesn't have authority over language, but language—that is, a spoken statement—is determined by chance and fragility. The speaker simultaneously steps out of speechless anonymity, enters the public sphere, and makes himself and his personhood a topic for public scrutiny.[19] His statement can turn into a lie, just as his oath can turn into perjury or his promise can become an untruth because man hasn't been granted sovereignty over language. In a performative statement, as presented par excellence in an oath or a promise, an interpersonal reality can be created that closely connects the statement of the person, who is making a promise or swearing an oath, with his own personhood and exposes him to acknowledgment by the Other. In order for such a new reality, created through language, to have an effect on the world, the recipient (an individual or a collective, such as a nation or a community of fellow believers) has to accept it as a condition for the performance of each respective statement.[20] Just as language cannot directly reproduce external reality, an oath has likewise little direct effect on an interpersonal relationship; an oath only becomes effective when it is also considered believable by the other person. This requires the

18. See Giorgio Agamben, *The Sacrament of Language: An Archaeology of the Oath*, trans. Adam Kotsko (Stanford, CA: Stanford University Press, 2011), 71.
19. See Searle, *Making the Social World*, 83. Even if fragility is an essential element of language, and working with it doesn't always come easily to man, language does have an enormous potential to restrict and torture him. Žižek seems to exaggerate this point when he speaks of "The Torture-House of Language" and barely pays attention to its creative aspects. See Slavoj Žižek, "The Torture-House of Language," in *Less Than Nothing: Hegel and the Shadow of Dialectical Materialism* (London: Verso, 2012), 869–78.
20. See Searle, *Making the Social World*, 76, 84–86.

recipient to have trust (Greek: *pistis*) in the words and actions of the speaking, swearing person as well as in this person himself.[21]

If the recipient doesn't trust the other person, or trust his actions and statements, then there is no relationship of acknowledgment and trust between the speaker and the recipient. The statement won't be accepted as true (i.e., as the truth) because the recipient doesn't believe in any correspondence or agreement between the speaker's words and the given reality—that is, what is expected in the future. The recipient will see an insurmountable gap between the words and the corresponding reality that, under certain circumstances, may still have to prove itself or become manifest, and this can turn the statement into a falsehood.[22] The primacy of the given reality, or what is expected in the future, is especially relevant here. Man can't substantially alter his given reality through words in such a way that words would give him sovereignty over reality.[23] According to Searle, as soon as man makes a statement, he presents himself before the public because by turning toward a counterpart, he breaks his preverbal stance of isolation: "To see why, we have to see that the speech act is more than just the expression of an intention or the expression of a belief. *It is above all a public performance.* I am telling something to someone else. But I am not just telling him that I have a belief or that I have an intention; I am telling him something about the world represented by those beliefs and intentions. By committing myself to the conditions of satisfaction of the belief (in making a statement), I am telling him that this is how the world is."[24]

In the speech act, the speaker presents his view and his understanding of the world. The individual's original perspective is brought to light and is introduced to the world. According to Gadamer, man presents his own provisional world horizon, his prejudgment. However, it is subject to the condition that it will be constantly revised and expanded on through new experiences so that it can make

21. See Agamben, *Sacrament*, 26–27, 65.
22. Correspondence theory has been a fundamental component in the analysis of the essence of truth since antiquity; in this context, it means that a declarative statement must, by necessity, correspond to the named reality. See Aristotle, *Metaphysics*, in Barnes, *Complete Works of Aristotle*, vol. 2: "It is not because we think that you are white, that you *are* white, but because you are white we who say this have the truth" (1661 [1051b]).
23. Even the performative statement of an insult only has a "reality-creating" characteristic when the insulted person has a personal relationship to the speaker of the insult. If the insulted person, strictly speaking, is indifferent toward the speaker, the effect of the insult fizzles, and it can't serve the function of an invective or humiliation. The insulting statement has no effect in regard to its relationship with reality.
24. Searle, *Making the Social World*, 83–84.

hermeneutical progress in concept formation and in the epistemological process, because no provisional horizon and no prejudgment should be static.[25] When man presents his prejudgment of the world, to a certain extent, he unmasks himself and subjects his prejudgment to scrutiny. His statement is thus inextricably linked with his personhood. Giorgio Agamben, following Michel Foucault, says—in fact, he must say—that man, in regard to a human speech situation, is "*the living being whose language places his life in question.*"[26] For man, on the one hand, speech is a precarious situation in which he differentiates himself as a human being, but on the other hand, when he speaks, he puts his personhood, and the acknowledgment that comes along with it, at stake.[27]

25. See Gadamer, *Truth and Method*, 102–4. See also Gadamer: "In fact our own prejudice is properly brought into play by being put at risk. Only by being given full play is it able to experience the other's claim to truth and make it possible for him to have full play himself" (299).
26. Agamben, *Sacrament*, 69.
27. See Agamben, 71.

2

God's Initiative

God's Intrusion into Man's Horizon of Understanding

Prolegomena to a View of God in the Twenty-First Century

The history of Western theology also supports the claim that one's historical horizon determines one's prejudgment and view of the world. The Enlightenment and critics of religion, such as Ludwig Feuerbach, Karl Marx, and Friedrich Nietzsche, are evidence of a clear historical break that made it possible, and required, man's view of God to be reevaluated. The effects of this critique of religion on Western intellectual life have continued: Richard Dawkins is a paradigmatic example[1] of this ongoing confrontation between theology and spirited questioning and theology's need to continue to respond to this kind of critique.

The questions that are important today are these: "In what way?" "To what end?" and "What kind of progress?" If two irreconcilable stances—with nothing in common—were to confront each other, it would be difficult for them to make any hermeneutic progress. It should also be noted here that even Nietzsche—he proclaimed the death of God with, perhaps, the deepest passion of all humanity—had to admit to his own limited perspective in the following comparatively succinct comment: "At bottom, it is only the moral god that has been overcome."[2]

1. See Richard Dawkins, *The God Delusion* (Boston: Houghton Mifflin, 2006).
2. Friedrich Nietzsche, *The Will to Power*, ed. Walter Kaufmann, trans. Walter Kaufmann and R. J. Hollingdale (New York: Random House, 1967), 36. See Peter Köster, "Gott," in *Nietzsche-Handbuch: Leben—Werk—Wirkung*, ed. Henning Ottmann (Stuttgart, Germany: J. B. Metzler, 2011), 245–48. See also Jean-Luc Marion, *God without Being: Hors-Texte*, trans. Thomas A. Carlson, with a foreword by David Tracy (Chicago: University of Chicago Press, 2012), 16. Although Jean-Luc Marion's interpretation of this passage does not correspond to the general Nietzsche reception and interpretation, its compatibility with theology is sufficient grounds to consider it productive for theological-philosophical discourse.

In this passage, Nietzsche only refers to the overcoming of a moral God because this is the primary presupposition of his own philosophy of a higher human presence (Dasein); this has left him constrained by a man-made but extremely confining system of values. From here, Nietzsche dares to find a path to the "Superman-Presence" (Übermenschen-Dasein), while the human perspective toward truth remains trapped in error and inadequacy and doesn't have the strength on its own to subject its own perspective to its own will.

Nietzsche shows great skepticism in his response to the question of how man acknowledges the reality of the world through his cognitive achievements. Using the language of a fable, "On Truth and Lie in an Extra-Moral Sense" begins, "In some remote corner of the universe, poured out and glittering in innumerable solar systems, there once was a star on which clever animals invented knowledge. That was the haughtiest and most mendacious minute of 'world history'—yet only a minute. After nature had drawn a few breaths the star grew cold, and the clever animals had to die."[3]

Man appears to Nietzsche as an animal that possesses no objective grasp of the reality of Being (Seinswirklichkeit) in matters of knowledge but instead attributes to himself a position that has no basis in reality; strictly speaking, man's claim to possess knowledge about reality is only wishful thinking. This claim is an illusory self-deception in which man places himself in a position above reality in order to avoid being dominated by reality. To be sure, Nietzsche is not a philosopher who builds systems in which individual writings, thoughts, and images fit tightly together into a coherent, consistent, meaningful whole. Nietzsche's answer to the question of why man wants and must take this position is based on his own relationship to the truth of reality:

> It is shameful for a philosopher to say, "the good and the beautiful are one"; if he adds to this, "also the true," he ought to be thrashed. Truth is ugly. We *have art*, so we don't perish from the truth. . . .

3. Friedrich Nietzsche, "On Truth and Lie in an Extra-Moral Sense," in *The Portable Nietzsche*, trans. Walter Kaufmann (New York: Viking, 1954), 42. See Claus Zittel, "Erkenntnis," in Ottmann, *Nietzsche-Handbuch*, 219–20.

> The birth of tragedy believes in art as the background of another belief: that it's *impossible to live with the truth*; that the "Will to Truth" is already a symptom of degeneration.[4]

For man, truth isn't something that is easy to manage; he is unable to bring it under his sovereignty. Man can't mold the truth into a form such that it is subordinate to him—the truth frightens him. If man doesn't want to take a stance of concealment toward the truth, he will be shown "the truth about the sadness and meaninglessness of *Dasein* . . . in its monstrous brutality."[5] Beautiful appearances are necessary for man's survival—that is, for the survival of the last man, who is unable to reveal the truth to himself and whose stance toward the truth doesn't make any space available to it. The truth remains concealed for reasons of self-defense.

This reading of Nietzsche should not create the impression that he was secretly—whether unconsciously or not—a person who was seeking God but couldn't or didn't want to admit to it. Nietzsche was not that kind of person.[6] For him, God was irrevocably dead; one mustn't forget this. Theology should nonetheless take to heart the task of inquiring into the kind of God that men are engaged with, if man's view of God serves as the definitive standard. This God is dead because he didn't live, because he was never divine, and because he could only act within the horizon that the human gaze made available to him.[7] This God is a human *idol*; the human perspective has set limits on him. The human gaze allows God to become a concept and be summarized in a concept; it makes God into a thing that man can (intelligibly) *grasp*.[8] This idolatrous concept of God doesn't allow for a transcendent, invisible reality that can't be enclosed in man's gaze and horizon. The reality of a God intruding from the outside, beyond man's limiting

4. Friedrich Nietzsche, *Sämtliche Werke: Kritische Studienausgabe in 15 Bänden*, ed. Giorgio Colli and Mazzino Montinari, vol. 13, *Nachgelassene Fragmente*: 1887–1889 (Munich, Germany: Deutscher Taschenbuch Verlag / de Gruyter, 1999), 500.
5. Konrad Paul Liessmann, *Schönheit* (Vienna: Facultas.wuv, 2009), 43–44.
6. See Köster, "Gott," 245.
7. See Marion, *God*: "The gaze alone makes the idol, as the ultimate function of the gazeable" (10).
8. See Marion: "When a philosophical thought expresses a concept of what it then names 'God,' this concept functions exactly as an idol. It gives itself to be seen, but thus all the better conceals itself as the mirror where thought, invisibly, has its forward point fixed, so that the *invisable* finds itself, with an aim suspended by the fixed concept, disqualified and abandoned; thought freezes, and the idolatrous concept of 'God' appears, where, more than God, thought judges itself" (16). See Marion, 29–33, 57.

gaze, can't be tolerated by this gaze that is the manifestation of a stance toward the divine.[9] Man can manage a divine idol that is both harmless and nonthreatening. This God has become static and emptied of his divinity; his God-Being (Gottsein) has been removed and overcome. Theologians should give Nietzsche credit for being right on this point, and they should take the resulting, implicit warning seriously so as not to fall into an unconscious atheism of an idolatrous kind due to methodological objectivity, because God, the idol, is no longer a God.

In principle, even a pious theologian is susceptible to the danger of idolatry because it protects man from having to tolerate any of the imponderables and irrational states of uncertainty that a divine God, in his acknowledged divinity, expects. Gazing at God in this way limits him. In order to counteract the danger of idolatry and man's limited perspective toward God that is associated with it, it is incumbent upon man not to take up his own perspective toward God but rather to accept a point of view that has been granted and made possible by God. Instead of viewing God as firmly fixed in the visible world and blocking any view that goes beyond the surface, the iconic gaze provides an opening so that God himself can appear to man beyond visible reality. The visible is only a hinge, a window, or a mediated means for communicating this gaze of iconic openness. Through the iconic gaze, God can appear to man and thereby determine the parameters of his image and also, independently, set limits on how he presents himself to man: "The icon does not result from a vision but provokes one."[10] Through man's iconic gaze, the visible surface becomes permeable to the surplus character of the divine; man mustn't set any arbitrary limits on the divine if God, in his initial gesture toward man, wants to inform man of his existence.

In the idolatrous stance, the visible becomes a mirror for man because he is the one who determines whether there is a reality beyond the visible; man answers this question in the negative—with a no—claiming that *his own interpretive authority alone sets the visible surface* as the standard of the real. The gaze of openness greatly diminishes man's interpretive authority by placing him in a submissive posture. Man's reverence for God's greatness expands his horizon so that his

9. See Marion, 13.
10. Marion, 17.

prejudgment about God's intrusion into human reality can be revised; man can now hear God's message:[11]

> If man, by his gaze, renders the idol possible, in reverent contemplation of the icon, on the contrary, the gaze of the invisible, in person, aims at man. The icon regards us—it *concerns* us, in that it allows the intention of the invisible to occur visibly. . . . The icon opens in a face, where man's sight envisages nothing, but goes back infinitely from the visible to the invisible by the grace of the visible itself: instead of the invisible mirror, which sent the human gaze back to itself alone and censured the *invisible*, the icon opens in a face that gazes at our gazes in order to summon them to its depth.[12]

In the idolatrous stance, the gaze transforms everything that is presented to it in such a way that the surface becomes static, and one can't infer greater depth. In contrast, a transcendent, structural excess is part of the openness of the iconic gaze, and it can give rise to a receptive experience that is much greater than a view of what is visible. To the contrary, in the icon, the visible indirectly presents the material manifestation of man's inability to understand.[13]

God's Intrusion into the World of the Israelites

The First Vatican Council declared, as a matter of doctrine, that there is reasonable plausibility to have faith in a God who is considered the cause and purpose of all Being (Sein; DH, 3004, DH, 3026). Without this plausibility of faith, one disavows its basic foundation (Rom 1:19–20; 1 Pet 3:15) and surrenders faith and everything related to it to pure irrationality. Without rational proof, the idea of God would

11. See Marion, 19. See Gadamer, *Truth and Method*: "Rather, a person trying to understand a text is prepared for it to tell him something. That is why a hermeneutically trained consciousness must be, from the start, sensitive to the text's alterity. But this kind of sensitivity involves neither 'neutrality' with respect to content nor the extinction of one's self, but the foregrounding and appropriation of one's own fore-meanings and prejudices. The important thing is to be aware of one's own bias, so that the text can present itself in all its otherness and thus assert its own truth against one's own fore-meanings" (271–72). What is noted here in regard to the ability to understand a secular text will later also be applied to a biblical text over the course of this investigation.
12. Marion, *God*, 19.
13. See Marion, 21–23.

lack a meaningful explanation for the entirety of Being (Seinsganzen). It must therefore be noted that the human perspective is the decisive criterion determining the direction of this investigation: It begins with man. It should be obvious that this is not, by any means, a result of an imperfect view of man's movement toward knowledge; it stems from the fact that a horizon must first exist before it can be expanded. Man must have *preconditioned* knowledge—even if it's incorrect—so that it can be revised.[14] In this context, expanding and revising *preconditioned* knowledge is a subsequent step. Even Jean-Luc Marion, who argues vehemently on behalf of reverence for an idol and man's gaze upon it, admits that the idol does not primarily deceive man but rather presents everything, unabridged, that is visible through the superficiality of sense perception.[15] This means that the idolatrous gaze can, in effect, be put aside so that the icon takes in the gaze of the spectator to the extent that the spectator is gazed upon by the icon.[16] An evental site—that is, a bounded horizon—is needed so that an external event can enter into it; the concrete situation that found its location at this site can then lead to an altered situation.[17] For example, the absolute state of the ancien régime in France was necessary so that France could later be changed by the French Revolution. A situation or *preconditioned* knowledge is therefore indispensable for an external intrusion into reality in order to correct *preconditioned* knowledge.

In this regard, one must examine the biblical basis for the claim that the revelation of God (i.e., God's name) was, to a certain extent, imposed upon man from the outside; this examination is absolutely necessary for a Christian theologian because sacred Scripture is the fundamental and standard testimony for the church (DV 10, 975) because this is where God himself appears. In the description of this event in Exodus, when God summons Moses, God turns to Moses and through him to the Israelites. God doesn't only reveal his name; in addition to disclosing his name, God makes a statement about his being, saying that he was already the God of Moses's ancestors and that he will continue to prove himself to be a faithful God to his adopted people (Exod 3:15). In this way, God ties his actions on behalf of the ancestors and the Israelites together; this creates a sense of continuity despite

14. See Gadamer, *Truth and Method*, 278, 294.
15. See Marion, *God*, 9–14.
16. See Marion, 19.
17. See Alain Badiou, *Being and Event*, trans. Oliver Feltham (London: Continuum, 2006), 174–77.

the enormous time difference. What's most important to note here is that when God makes the statement about himself—"I will be whoever I will be" (Exod 3:14)[18]—God doesn't answer Moses's question directly as to what his name is (i.e., who he really is). God gives Moses an opportunity to prove to the Israelites that he has been sent as God's emissary; Moses promises his people a perspective on what is to come in the future that will prove that he will also be the God of this people.[19]

It must be emphasized here that (1) God will continue to remain inaccessible to man, despite his promise of proof as to what is to come in the future and the hope that this gives the Israelites, and (2) God alone has the freedom to make decisions about his being and actions throughout history.[20] Moses's question about God's name is apropos, especially in a polytheistic context, as a way to differentiate this God, who has adopted his own group, from the other surrounding gods. However, God's separation from the surrounding world is not the most striking aspect of this passage; more importantly, God shows his solidarity with this group when he approaches them and opens up the possibility of a personal encounter with them by revealing his name.[21]

Although God's statement about his name and actions appears to be a tautological statement that does not make logical sense, this statement illustrates God's inaccessibility to man in an especially succinct way because it is essential to God's sovereignty that he alone makes assertions about himself and his actions throughout history. God doesn't define himself here in order to establish his essence in a static form; in this context, it is more important to emphasize God's self-determined closeness to history[22] and to note that it is part of God's plan to

18. This literal translation is based on Georg Fischer and Dominik Markl, *Das Buch Exodus* (Stuttgart, Germany: Katholisches Bibelwerk, 2009), 54, 58. (Translator's note: *The New Oxford Annotated Bible* translates this phrase as "I AM WHO I AM." Fischer and Markl include an extensive discussion of translation issues regarding Exodus 3 [54–58]; see also notes on this passage in *The New Oxford Annotated Bible*.)
19. See Helmut Utzschneider and Wolfgang Oswald, *Exodus 1–15: International Exegetical Commentary on the Old Testament* (IEKAT), trans. Philip Sumpter (Stuttgart, Germany: Verlag W. Kohlhammer, 2015), 123–24.
20. See Fischer and Markl, *Exodus*, 54. Regarding the one-sidedness—on God's part—of the beginning of this joint relationship, see Josef Schreiner, *Theologie des Alten Testaments* (Würzburg, Germany: Echter Verlag, 1995): "No phrasing exists that would suggest that Israel would initiate a relationship with God through wording similar to the following: We are (will be) your people, Yahweh, and you are (will become) our God. We can only appeal to what God previously said, voluntarily enacted, and decreed" (53).
21. See Klaus Grünwaldt, *Gott und sein Volk: Die Theologie der Bibel* (Darmstadt, Germany: Wissenschaftliche Buchgesellschaft, 2006), 23–24.
22. See Utzschneider and Oswald, *Exodus 1–15*, 124.

choose his own people and to act on their behalf throughout history. In this passage, a dialectic connection comes to light in the relationship between God and man. On the one hand, God remains inaccessible to man; Moses can't look directly at God—the burning bush is an epiphanic phenomenon—even though Moses may and also wants to look at the bush. And according to the Bible, a direct sighting of God leads to a man's death (Exod 33:20).[23] On the other hand, God reveals his name to Moses and promises to treat him as divine. This dialectic of proximity and distance is a God-given rapprochement in which God takes the initiative because man, in his horizon, doesn't have the sovereignty to get closer to God on his own; God gets closer to man by revealing his name to him.

According to ancient Eastern beliefs, knowing a person's name could make it possible to wield power and have sovereignty over that person, in certain respects. A name was not simply a name that was given to a person and then subsequently and arbitrarily connected to the name; rather, the name belonged by definition to the essence of the person and wasn't a secondary attribute that was subsequently added.[24] Thus the name of a person could be inserted into an oath, and the person could thereby be cursed in an (quasi-magical) oath-swearing ritual. This is one way to treat a name, and it opens up the possibility of misusing it to one's own advantage. In contrast, knowing God's name is precisely what makes it possible to address prayers to God, to express one's personal gratitude to him, and to hold a ritual that commemorates God's acts of salvation.[25] Fischer and Markl write the following about the significance of naming: "God's explicitly stated wish, as in Ex 3:15, that not only is Yahweh his name, but that he be remembered for eternity, likewise deserves consideration. The naming of his name (Ex 3:4) establishes a *personal relationship*, more than a title or a role would. God wants to be closely enough connected to us humans that we can address him familiarly."[26]

Man must also reciprocate this gift that God has given him; only in this way, by being able to express God's name in sentences, does man still lack sovereignty

23. See Otto Kaiser, *Der Gott des Alten Testaments: Wesen und Wirken; Theologie des Alten Testaments, Teil 2: Jahwe, der Gott Israels, Schöpfer der Welt und des Menschen* (Göttingen, Germany: Vandenhoeck & Ruprecht, 1998), 93–95.
24. See Isaiah 43:1: "But now thus says the Lord, he who created you, O Jacob, he who formed you, O Israel: Do not fear, for I have redeemed you; I have called you by name, you are mine." See also Isaiah 45:4.
25. See Utzschneider and Oswald, *Exodus 1–15*, 125.
26. Fischer and Markl, *Exodus*, 57.

over God. However, man does have the opportunity that has been granted to Moses to confirm the nature of the relationship that God has opened up to him, man can respond to God, and man can subsequently continue this relationship if he so desires. The ostensibly tautological statement in Exodus 3:14 reinforces the fact that Moses is certainly entitled to communicate God's will and name with authority; however, only God alone may speak definitively about himself and his acts of salvation: "He alone can make accurate and definitive statements about himself, and he offers access to his essence by revealing his name. In the process, the specific form of his announcement in Exodus 3:14 makes it clear that his name is not to be used like a magic spell that would have sovereignty over him; God's freedom and inaccessibility are guaranteed, even when he has granted them."[27] God opens up a space for shared communication so that (1) the Israelites know who has reached out to them; (2) there is still a possibility, through the revelation of God's name, for the Israelites to respond to God's offer to speak; and (3) the Israelites, in this situation of solidarity, also have the opportunity to bring their own requests and concerns to God. God's quasi-tautological statement about his name should also immediately bring an end to any of man's illusions that he has access to magical powers. This reinforces the fact that man doesn't have the sovereignty over God to force him into a verbal formula that, through its ritual character, could influence the future through magic. Man is neither entitled to such power nor able to acquire it by force. Man should respect God's name because he would otherwise misjudge God's turning toward him for solidarity. In order to put an end to such a request, and to show man the danger of such a plan—he would, in effect, be tempting God (Deut 6:16)—the Decalogue doesn't allow for any ambiguity regarding a person's attitude toward God's name:[28] "You shall not make wrongful use of the name of the Lord your God, for the Lord will not acquit anyone who misuses his name" (Exod 20:7). Man shouldn't have a narcissistic attitude toward God; as the preamble to the Decalogue (Exod 20:2) reminds him, man would then also misjudge God's chosen actions of liberation on his own behalf.[29]

27. Fischer and Markl, 58.
28. See Grünwaldt, *Gott*, 24.
29. See Fischer and Markl, *Exodus*, 224–26.

Following the narrative line of the Exodus story, Moses's experience—that is, the Israelites' experience with YHWH—doesn't end with the revelation of God's name. God opens up to Moses and the Israelites the possibility of a dialogue that is focused on God's name. God's name becomes, in a manner of speaking, a guarantor or a seal; it confirms that God has adopted his people, has recognized their suffering, and will accompany them in the future. Even when YHWH says that the ancestors knew his name, God counters by saying that he did not reveal his identity to them—that is, he did not offer them this quality of experience. And they, to a certain extent, weren't able to experience God in all his divinity.[30] To be sure, there are passages before this event in Exodus where YHWH introduces himself by name and reveals himself (Gen 28:13).[31] However, even when he, as an agent of God's revelation, announces God's name, and even though this particular person is close to YHWH, he has been informed that it is a signifier of God. In this context, God's introduction of himself has a fundamentally different quality. It is part of God's sovereignty to determine the signified of his name, semantically-qualitatively, so that man's horizon of experience and understanding, in regard to his relationship with God, will be redefined, and it will also know no limits due to the infinite, incomprehensible greatness of God:[32]

> Then God talked and spoke to Moses:
>   "I am YHWH.

30. See Utzschneider and Oswald, *Exodus 1–15*:

> However, the emphasis of the passage is less on the announcement of the name as such and more on the intensity and quality of the experience of the divine bearer of the name. . . . The claim in Exod 6:2 that God had *not* made himself known to the Patriarchs under the name YHWH has the positive implication that when YHWH does present himself under this name it will entail an experience of God that is qualitatively new in comparison to what has been experienced thus far. The reference to the period of the Patriarchs is thus simultaneously a reference to the liminality of the situation in which the speech is taking place. (159)

31. See Horst Seebass, *Genesis II: Vätergeschichten II (23.1–36.43)* (Neukirchen-Vluyn, Germany: Neukirchener Verlag, 1999), 312–17.
32. According to Lacan's fundamental, structural model of human reality, the empty name (pure signifier) is the high point of his legal, ordered dimension. This explains why Lacan, following Freud, also calls this empty name the "Name-of-the-Father" and determines, likewise following Freud, that this is the intersection of man's view of the structure of Being (Seinsgefüge). The empty signifier is necessary but also indeterminate. See also Dylan Evans, *An Introductory Dictionary of Lacanian Psychoanalysis* (London: Routledge, 1996), 119, 182–84. See also Jacques Lacan, *The Psychoses: The Seminar of Jacques Lacan*, bk. 3, 1955–1956, ed. Jacques-Alain Miller, trans. Russell Grigg (New York: W. W. Norton, 1993): "Experience proves it—the more the signifier signifies nothing, the more indestructible it is" (185).

> I appeared to Abraham, Isaac, and Jacob as El Shaddai, I did not make myself known to them, however, by the name of YHWH. I also established my covenant with them to give them the land of Canaan, the land of their foreign residence, in which they were foreigners. And I, yes I have heard the groaning of the Israelites, whom the Egyptians have made subservient, and I have remembered my covenant."
>
> Therefore say to the Israelites:
>
> "I am YHWH.
>
> And will (therefore) lead you out from under the burdens of Egypt, liberate you from servitude, and redeem you with an outstretched arm and great acts of judgment.
>
> I will take you to be my people and I will be your God, so that you recognize that I am YHWH, your God who leads you out from under the burdens of Egypt.
>
> I will bring you into the land concerning which I have raised my hand to give it to Abraham, Isaac, and Jacob. And I will give it to you for a possession.
>
> I am YHWH."[33]

The experiences of the Israelites, especially those of the ancestors, can't be logically deduced in such a way that similar experiences with God in the future can simply be carried out and foretold ahead of time. Man's horizon always remains limited and trapped in a static situation as long as he doesn't experience any additional intrusion from the outside. God's sovereignty over man is particularly evident here because God is the one who will make decisions about the future experience of the Israelites, depending on how he presents himself to them. God's announcement of his name to Moses—on the surface, it appears to be a tautological statement—makes it extremely clear that it is God's plan alone that will determine how he will present himself to the Israelites and thereby alter their horizon.[34] The signifier (God's name) remains the same, but its qualitative content (statements about God's being

33. Translation of Exodus 6:2–8 based on Utzschneider and Oswald, *Exodus 1–15*, 157.
34. See Fischer and Markl, *Exodus*, 91.

and actions) is, from a human perspective, limitless—that is, inexhaustible;[35] hence man can't define God.

It is not always a new experience that opens up man's horizon and leads him to a new, revised position. An experience *can* be so all-encompassing that it will continue to influence man's horizon. This kind of experience will shift man's point of view into a state of dynamic instability, and his reflections about the reality he has experienced will be lasting and continue to develop. Thus Exodus 3–4 is the only passage where God reveals his name and presents it as a continuation of his historical acts on behalf of the ancestors;[36] no insularity is intended for the common path of God and the Israelites (i.e., it can't be easily determined). Rather, Israel's future prospects are opened up through this personal relationship that is closely linked to the past. By revealing his name, it appears that God wants to be remembered by the people he has adopted. By revealing his name, he accompanies his people and makes it possible for them to speak to him personally and to address their own prayers to him. God isn't only part of their contemporary experience but also remains alive in their memory:[37] "And God spoke again to Moses: 'This is how you should speak to the Israelites: "YHWH, the God of your fathers, the God of Abraham, the God of Isaac, and the God of Jacob, has sent me to you. This is my name for ever and this is how I will be commemorated from generation to generation."'"[38]

By announcing his name (it was God's own decision to reveal it to the Israelites), he made it possible for the Israelites to recognize God's historically significant guidance over the course of time without, in any way, simultaneously diminishing God's transcendence and detachment and thereby—as it were—his divinity in the least. The name that God revealed became a marker of God's presence amid his

35. Jean-François Lyotard also denies the possibility of attaining (even limited) knowledge of God through the revelation of his name based on epistemology subsequent to Kant and the sublime. A name is nothing more than a trace and a clue. To the contrary, it is much more a mark of epistemological absence, as Wendel writes, "Another trace is a name as a way to present the 'nameless' because a name lacks meaning; from a purely formal perspective, it is a 'fixed designator,' as Lyotard explains, following Saul Kripke. A name can therefore point to something, without wanting to define it, but it also unable to represent it. In particular, YHWH is this kind of name; it is the ineffable name that isn't the name of a divine being, but, by being unnamable, it is a trace, a mark of the likewise unnamable Absolute." Saskia Wendel, "'Nichtsprechendes Sprechen' über Transzendenz: Lyotard—Derrida—Levinas," in *Wie lässt sich über Gott sprechen? Von der negativen Theologie Plotins bis zum religiösen Sprachspiel Wittgensteins*, ed. Werner Schüssler (Darmstadt, Germany: Wissenschaftliche Buchgesellschaft, 2008), 276.
36. See Fischer and Markl, *Exodus*, 47.
37. See Fischer and Markl, 55.
38. Translation of Exodus 3:15 is based on Utzschneider and Oswald, *Exodus* 1–15, 122.

people; the name could bridge the dialectic of proximity and distance and transcendence and immanence, and it could bind them together in simultaneity. God's revelation of his name, through grace, could thereby be recognized as a permanent seal of God's proximity and devotion to his people.

God's outreach to the Israelites doesn't lead to a forced bond between them; God's announcement of his name and promise of future assistance is an offer, on God's part, to converse with the Israelites. For man, it is imperative for the success of the exodus that the Israelites listen to God's message and accept it—that is, act in accordance with it. God himself takes the initiative for their being together (Zusammensein), jointly, when he intrudes into man's horizon in a welcoming way. The acceptance of God's invitation to be together in community and to listen to God's instructions isn't mandatory because Israel can also turn away from God:

> Listening is a prerequisite for God's act of salvation to have an effect. Refusing to listen to him is an attack on him and is followed by punishment. His demands serve his people in the very best way possible. Everyone must obey them and carry them out.
>
> The instructions that Yahweh issues are not arbitrary demands or capricious orders that have assembled. . . . Yahweh doesn't just demand something so that Israel can show and prove its obedience. He is responsive to Israel's needs and life. This remains fundamentally the same throughout the history of God's people.[39]

The purpose of God's instructions is not to demand blind obedience but rather to show that the Lord looks after his people and takes care of their needs. God's commandments and instructions to the Israelites stem from his concern for them, and they are in their best interests.[40]

God's decision to reveal his name to his people, based on his counsel, opened up the possibility of accessibility and spiritual closeness; it can therefore be viewed as one of the principal roots of the Deuteronomistic connection between the theology

39. Schreiner, *Theologie*, 100–101.
40. The Lord's instructions will subsequently lead to a transformation in human practices and social solidarity so that inner-directed faith and religious practices in a social environment can only be separated from another with great difficulty: "For I desire steadfast love and not sacrifice, the knowledge of God rather than burnt offerings" (Hos 6:6).

of name and temple. God's actions, through grace, on behalf of his people brought about the reassessment of their hermeneutic horizon; his actions were the decisive impetus for a more suitable relationship between the Israelites and their God. According to the narrative line of the Pentateuch, the wandering Israelites, who had experienced their exodus out of Egyptian bondage to the promised land—"a land flowing with milk and honey" (Exod 3:17)—became, under God's guidance, a sedentary people with a central holy shrine in Jerusalem, where his name dwells in the temple. God chose the Israelites and led them to the promised land because he had shown them his solidarity by initiating a sense of community with them and by revealing his name to them; this opened up the possibility of a communicative exchange in which God's transcendence wouldn't be attacked, but he also wouldn't be confronting Israel from an insurmountable distance. The revelation of his name is the moment of revelation and encounter within the world: "By revealing his name, he confirms that he is present, active, and effective."[41]

God's actions toward his people are not *primarily* recognized as an abstract plan of salvation that is visible to man. Because God, despite all the transgressions of his people, doesn't break this bond and his promise of salvation, and continues to treat them with generosity, the Israelites can, upon reflection, recognize God's large-scale, eternal acts of salvation on their behalf. God's will can't be fully comprehended, but God's actions on behalf of his people—such as his choosing his people, the exodus, the granting of land, or the return to Israel after the Babylonian exile—show that God treats his people with continuous steadfastness.[42] God's treatment of the Israelites is always in their best interest; therefore, God appeals to pedagogical methods, even when the Israelites deviate from the right path, so that his people can learn to recognize and correct their errors. It should be emphasized here that even the Israelites' greatest trespasses don't lead to the breaking of this covenant and his promise because God keeps his word (Ps 33:4, 11: "For the word of the Lord is upright, and all his work is done in faithfulness. . . . The counsel of the Lord stands forever, the thoughts of his heart to all generations").

It is also clear from God's treatment of the Israelites that a name is closely related to a person's being, according to ancient Eastern beliefs: the honor of his own name leads God to overlook the Israelites' transgressions in the exile event

41. Schreiner, *Theologie*, 38.
42. See Schreiner, 76–78.

and, for the sake of his own name, to forgive the trespasses of his people (Isa 48:9), even though the Israelites don't give God any reason to turn toward them again (Isa 43:22–25; Ezek 20:44; 36; 22–23). God's name isn't only a label that gives humans a way to address him in person. His name is, by definition, an element of his being. God's name carries so much weight because it is so closely connected to his being; this also explains why it is such a great concern in Judaism to honor God's name, not to misuse it, and not to take his name in vain.[43]

It wasn't necessary for God to reveal his name to the Israelites; therefore, the fact that they were permitted to know God's name mustn't be dismissed as something banal in the history of salvation. This is solely, and exclusively, based on God's freely chosen divine counsel; he chose a people, he accompanied them throughout history, and he revealed his name to them as a sign of his personal covenant and his detached closeness to them.[44] Through the revelation of God's name, through grace, Israelites have a permanent seal of God's invisible presence.

By revealing his name, God's bond with the Israelites is not limited to the Exodus situation; it remained the true reality for the Israelites when they became a sedentary people and when the tabernacle provided them a central place for honoring God and for God's presence amid his people. According to the Deuteronomic perspective, after the Israelites' land was occupied, God also chose Zion in order to have a central location for his people and his (representative) presence. This was the place that he occupied not only through his name; it was also the place where he wanted his name to reside, in a dwelling that was yet to be constructed (Deut 12:1–11; 21). A topological theology is presented in this Deuteronomic theology of the tabernacle; by revealing his name, God can reside here and be present amid the Israelites without diminishing his inaccessibility and divinity. Hence his initial gesture to the Israelites brings them closer to him. According to this theology, God's name and God's glory (Hebrew: *kabod*)—this also resides in the tabernacle—are a guarantee of his presence among men.[45] The book of Psalms, therefore, includes this hopeful statement in the context of the theology of Zion: "And those who know

43. The attitude of great respect for God's name in Judaism is so far reaching that God's name was only spoken once a year in Jesus's time and only by the high priest at the temple on the Day of Reconciliation. See Fischer and Markl, *Exodus*, 56.
44. See Grünwaldt, *Gott*, 21.
45. See Peter Weimar, "Herrlichkeit Gottes. 1. Altes Testament, II. Frühjudentum," in *LThK*, vol. 5, cols. 21–23. See also Psalm 75:1 ("We give thanks to you, O God; we give thanks; your name is near. People tell of your wondrous deeds.") and Psalm 113.

your name put their trust in you, for you, O Lord, have not forsaken those who seek you" (Ps 9:10). God's abiding support of those who pray—that is, believers—is also evident in this psalm because those who pray, knowing God's name, can now address their prayers to him in person. God's name has been revealed to them, and they have acknowledged his revelation through grace. Their prayers, through the use of God's name, will also be accepted by the Almighty One and won't be left to the horrors of the chaotic and occasionally hostile everyday world:

> Those who love me, I will deliver;
> I will protect those who know my name.
> When they call to me, I will answer them;
> I will be with them in trouble,
> I will rescue them and honor them. (Ps 91:14–15)

Deuteronomic theology views the Exodus event from the current situation of the Israelites (i.e., the tabernacle has already been destroyed), and through God's directive at that time, it recognizes that it was God's will that they build him a sacred tent and that God wanted a permanent dwelling amid his people that is allocated to and suitable for communication between him and his people (concerning the liturgy of atonement, see Exod 25:1–31 and especially Exod 25:8: "And have them make me a sanctuary, so that I may dwell among them"). Deuteronomic theology's role is to take God's invisible reality seriously and not create too strong a bond between God and the tabernacle; however, it must also not undermine God's simultaneous choice of the tabernacle as a central location for his presence amid the people of Israel or the historical significance of his guidance. Deuteronomic theology attempted to express the synthesis of this dialectic between proximity and distance, as well as presence and transcendence, by not locating God's presence in the tabernacle itself; instead, it referred to the dialectically mediated presence of God, whose name resides in the tabernacle.[46]

Even the destruction of the tabernacle in Jerusalem doesn't deny God's existence and his historical significance because God himself didn't reside in the tabernacle and wasn't dependent on a particular dwelling; the actual location of

46. See Bernd Janowski, *Gottes Gegenwart in Israel* (Neukirchen-Vluyn, Germany: Neukirchener Verlag, 1993), 128–29.

God's throne was in heaven. Despite God's choice to be close to his people, he preserved his freedom by revealing his name. And even the destruction of the tabernacle doesn't affect God's sovereignty in the slightest because the Israelites knew that the Babylonian exile was God's pedagogical punishment of his people (Isa 40:1–11). His people aren't far from him even when they leave Israel's borders because God's name indicates, communicates, and even denotes his presence. Therefore, a relationship with God is possible without a tabernacle because prayer offers believers the opportunity to experience God's presence.[47]

God's Self-Revelation through Jesus Christ

Given the discoveries of paleontology and the evidence supporting Charles Darwin's theory of evolution, it is no longer possible to defend a literal reading of the garden of Eden narrative in Genesis (Gen 2:4b–3:24) as a document of actual historical events. Interpreting paradise as a place of residence that actually once existed fails to recognize the biblical statement that underlies the shape of the narrative. At its core, the garden of Eden narrative is the great story of the origin of man and his current condition.[48] As is the case in many other biblical narratives, the main point of the story is found at the end, in the expulsion of man out of the garden of Eden and his banishment from his earlier carefree, privileged situation.[49] From a mythological horizon—that is, in mythological language—this is not the depiction of a real event; rather, following a Platonic understanding of myth, mythological language allows one to say something "that goes beyond the possibilities of an abstract presentation."[50] This is not the purpose of a purely logical, abstract theory. Myth can open up an ἱερός λόγος, "an ancient knowledge and view of essence that is unavailable to man"[51] and that would otherwise remain closed to him. Myth does not use strictly causal, naturalistic explanations to answer the question of the origin of a thing; to the contrary, through its linguistic form, it presents, comments upon, and verifies *current* conditions.[52]

47. See Janowski, 132.
48. See Christoph Dohmen, "Paradies. II. Biblisch-theologisch," in *LThK*, vol. 7, col. 1360.
49. See Horst Seebass, *Genesis I: Urgeschichte* (1.1–11.26) (Neukirchen-Vluyn, Germany: Neukirchener Verlag, 1996), 101.
50. Horst Bürkle, "Mythos, Mythologie, 1. Begriff., II. Religionsgeschichtlich," in *LThK*, vol. 7, col. 597.
51. Bürkle, col. 598.
52. See Bürkle, col. 598.

If one begins with this assumption and takes the peculiarities of mythological language or statements into account, then the garden of Eden narrative offers man an understandable and accessible answer to the question of why the creation is in principle good and just and why man nevertheless doesn't find himself in close proximity to God, his creator. Reality could be better than the reality man experiences today; human life is in a state of fragmentation and forlornness from its origin.[53] The garden of Eden narrative culminates in chapter 5:22, where man has the desire to be like God.[54]

In the garden of Eden narrative, man removes himself from God's immediacy; man wants to seize control over the interpretive authority of the plan of creation and does not want to accept the divine order unconditionally. This was not, in principle, envisioned in the plan of creation. Without offering any justification, man did not accept the situation that was granted to him; to the contrary, he doubted the order ordained by God and even mistrusted God.[55]

The following can, therefore, be considered as the quintessence of the garden of Eden narrative: man's detachment from God had not been envisioned in God's will for salvation. The story has therefore not lost its relevance for man in his current life: "Paradise continues to retain its permanent existential meaning as the truth about the salutary origin of man and its significance for the supernatural disposition of humanity."[56] However, because God's will for salvation is eternal and can't be altered through human behavior, God once again takes the initiative to open up a new possibility of directness, on his part, toward man. From a Christian perspective, this happened through the incarnation and God's self-revelation in Jesus Christ (John 1:1–4, 14).

In this context, God's initiative toward man, in which he offers himself to man through a new immediacy, does not take place at a moment of coercion or bondage. Therefore, the core of Jesus's proclamation doesn't consist in Jesus being the second person in an inner-Trinitarian event; rather, it marks the onset of the era of salvation and the unfolding of the current kingdom of God through his decree.

53. See Seebass, *Genesis* I, 102.
54. See Seebass, 102. Thus *hybris* (Latin: *superbia*) can be viewed as the foundation of all human sin, and man's own arrogance—that is, man's pride—becomes the defining factor in human action. See Wolfram Winger, "Hybris," in *LThK*, vol. 5, col. 350.
55. See Seebass, *Genesis* I, 102.
56. Leo Scheffezyk, "Paradies. III. Systematisch-theologisch," in *LThK*, vol. 7, col. 1362.

Thus Jesus's message doesn't focus on his incarnation—that is, that his incarnation would or should make up the entire content of his character. If one accepts the two-source hypothesis that the source Q and the Gospel of Mark were composed prior to Matthew and Luke, then the (historical) Jesus proclaims not his own majesty but rather the onset of the kingdom of God.[57] Even the sovereign title "Son of Man," which nobody except Jesus himself uses in the gospels, can only be applied indirectly to the person of Jesus because Jesus himself only speaks of the Son of Man in the third person. This raises the question—if one accepts the Son of Man logia of source Q as Jesus's ipsissima verba—as to whether Jesus was referring to himself by the title "Son of Man."[58] It is therefore only possible to apply this title to the person of Jesus indirectly.[59] Based on this reconstruction, it remains unclear (1) whether Jesus was referring to himself with this title; (2) whether this title in the third person was only a disguised statement in an Aramaic idiom that didn't mean anything other than "I"; or (3) whether Jesus, in this statement in the third person, was actually referring to another person, a third one.[60]

This remains undecidable as long as one limits one's inquiry to a field of supposed scientific objectivity or neutrality; it means that one isn't forced to accept Jesus as the Son of Man, who exists. This becomes extremely clear when Jesus, because of his message, is rejected, accused, and even given the disgraceful punishment of being nailed to the cross (Mark 14:55–65; 15:20–32). If Jesus's message had led his audience, through persuasion, to a new insight that left them no freedom of choice in their decision for or against him, they wouldn't have been able to reject him. This shows that grace and freedom are very closely connected to each other. God's turning toward man through grace has a threefold aspect as long as grace is understood as God's gift to man that is "freely given, unearned, and unable to be earned."[61] Through God's self-revelation in Jesus Christ by grace, man has the possibility to recognize his true humanity (Menschsein), and by accepting his true

57. The importance of this proclamation for the narrative is evident in Christ's first words in chapter 1 of the Gospel of Mark: "The time is fulfilled, and the kingdom of God has come near; repent, and believe in the good news" (Mark 1:15).
58. See Jürgen Becker, *Jesus of Nazareth*, trans. James E. Crouch (New York: Walter de Gruyter, 1998), 199–202. See also Paul Hoffmann, "Menschensohn. II. Neues Testament," in *LThK*, vol. 7, cols. 131–32.
59. See Becker, *Jesus*, 200.
60. See Becker, 201–2.
61. Bernd Jochen Hilberath, "F. Gnadenlehre," in *Handbuch der Dogmatik*, ed. Theodor Schneider (Düsseldorf, Germany: Patmos Verlag, 2000), 2:36.

humanity, he can get closer to God.[62] But if one understands "possibility" in the Aristotelian sense—as the potentiality that becomes evident precisely because it need not make *by necessity* the transition from potentiality to actuality but instead proves its potentiality by not being actualized in reality—then the essence of potentiality becomes evident in its existence as the intersection between actuality and lack of actuality.[63] Due to the incarnation, man is offered, to a certain extent, the possibility to decide on his own whether he will recognize Jesus as Christ and thus as fully empowered by God to allow the onset of the kingdom of God or whether he will reject him. Man is therefore in a position to decide whether to accept God's offer and Jesus's proclamation. A person of faith has already made this leap of faith and can see a greater reality behind a text than a surface reading of the text suggests, even if the text is conditioned by a particular historical period and is therefore limited. This means that the text of the gospels is not a time-limited, historical document that was written for a specific religious purpose; through the leap of faith, the text becomes Holy Scripture and, to a certain extent, an icon that remains relevant to the contemporary reality of the faithful.[64]

But the actual point here is to show that the core of Jesus's message doesn't concern him as a person, even though it depends on him (Luke 11:20); it concerns the onset and the unfolding of the kingdom of God as restitution for God's will for salvation in his divinely willed righteousness. This makes it clear that God's breaking into human reality and man's everyday world thwarts human rationality, which appears as foolishness to outsiders.[65] Thus John the Baptist, who, according to a classical-Christian perspective, prepares the way and proclaims Jesus's coming, possesses a diametrically opposed conceptual horizon, as will be seen in his

62. See Hilberath, 45.
63. See Aristotle, *Metaphysics*, 1659–60 (1050b–1051a). See also Otfried Höffe, *Aristotle*, trans. Christine Salazer (Albany: State University of New York Press, 2003), 73; and Giorgio Agamben, *Homo Sacer: Sovereign Power and Bare Life*, trans. Daniel Heller-Roazen (Stanford, CA: Stanford University Press, 1998):

> What is potential can pass over into actuality only at the point at which it sets aside its own potential not to be (its *adynamia*). To set impotentiality aside is not to destroy it but, on the contrary, to fulfill it, to turn potentiality back upon itself in order to give itself to itself. . . . Potentiality (in its double appearance as potentiality to and as potentiality not to) is that through which Being founds itself *sovereignly*, which is to say, without anything preceding or determining it (*superiorem non recognoscens*) other than its own ability not to be. And an act is sovereign when it realizes itself by simply taking away its own potentiality not to be, letting itself be, giving itself to itself. (46)

64. See Marion, *God*, 17.
65. See Marion, 63.

presentation of the onset of divine law and the kingdom of God. John the Baptist addresses his audience as a brood of vipers who can't escape divine judgment by fire. There is no longer time to repent because the ax is now lying at the root and the striking of God's judgment is at hand (Matt 3:1–12; 13:41–43; Luke 3:1–20). Putting aside the aftereffects of John the Baptist's teachings on Jesus,[66] it is clear from Jesus's proclamation that the kingdom of God has already begun. Jesus gives no warning before it is about to begin. Because the kingdom of God is unfolding in the present (Luke 11:20), man has to behave accordingly so that his actions stand in an appropriate relationship to God's merciful initiative toward him. This is illustrated in the Beatitudes, with their stance toward eschatology in the present. The mourners are already blessed in the present, precisely because they find comfort in the process as it unfolds, and those who are persecuted for their sacrificial actions for the sake of justice are already blessed in the present because the kingdom of God already belongs to them (Matt 5:4; 5:10).

One can see here, in the unfolding of God's will for salvation, that God is focusing on man's salvation. This explains why a large part of Jesus's work involves exorcism and healing of the sick and why he also accepts the outcasts of society (tax collectors and sinners, lepers, and the sick). They represent the paradigm of a sick person who is about to be healed: "'Those who are well have no need of a physician, but those who are sick; I have come to call not the righteous but sinners'" (Mark 2:17). In this way, Jesus, through his demands and actions, thwarts the horizon of expectation of the people, and they react with incomprehension and rejection (Matt 8:34; Mark 2:18–22; 10:43–45). God's acceptance of precisely those who have fallen (i.e., sinners) and those who are marginalized should also be the reason fellow human beings follow the example of Jesus—that is, God and his divine justice—and behave appropriately toward his emerging will for salvation. For this reason, one can also understand why Jesus, in a twofold commandment about love, places good behavior toward God right beside good behavior toward

66. One can also find aftereffects of John the Baptist's message of baptism in Jesus's words about future judgments by fire (see Matt 13:41–43, 49–50). But Jesus, John the Baptist's former student, rejects this perspective of the future kingdom of God and instead announces that the onset of the kingdom of God is already here (Matt 11:4–5: "Jesus answered them, 'Go and tell John what you hear and see: the blind receive their sight, the lame walk, the lepers are cleansed, the deaf hear, the dead are raised, and the poor have good news brought to them'").

one's fellow man.[67] Man does not love God if he separates God from God's will for salvation of his fellow human beings and keeps his relationship to God purely in the realm of the abstract and ill-defined. To a certain extent, man's *superbia* breaks fresh ground because he thereby reserves for himself interpretive authority. This limits God's will for salvation to the limits of man's horizon so that it doesn't cross the boundaries of what humans can comprehend. From this perspective, the existing situation remains the same for these people (i.e., unchanged) because they don't confront the rational, excessive character of the message of salvation—that the kingdom of God has come—with an attitude of openness.

God's will for salvation, given its divine dimension, goes in a direction that man can never fully fathom; therefore, man can never have complete insight. The Christian perspective possesses, or should possess, an openness toward the rational excessiveness of the event of God's salvation of man; to those outside this tradition, Jesus's suffering on the cross appears as foolishness and an irritation—that is, for Jews and Greeks, the event of the cross can't be brought into conformity with their religious horizon of expectation. Paul presents a contrast between a biased and therefore limited view of Christ's death on the cross and an attitude of openness toward the redemptive event. From a Greco-pagan perspective, the arrival or fulfillment of salvation could possibly have been recognized if it coincided with wisdom: it could mean salvation to Jews if it were authenticated and acknowledged by a sign from God (1 Cor 1:18–25).[68] For a person who isn't shaken by the message of salvation, despite supposed contradictions in this inner-worldly logic and rationality, and who, on the contrary, is open to being shown God's greatness in it and thus recognizes that the separation of human rationality and logic is being denounced on God's side, the event of the cross is the salvation of the world:[69] "But

67. Matthew 22:37–40: "'You shall love the Lord your God with all your heart, and with all your soul, and with all your mind.' This is the greatest and first commandment. And a second is like it: 'You shall love your neighbor as yourself.' On these two commandments hang all the law and the prophets."
68. Upon the arrival of the Messiah, one expected him to prove his identity through an extraordinarily miraculous deed that would certify his authenticity. This sign is not lacking, though "the power of God and the wisdom of God" (1 Cor 1:24) appear in a paradoxical way. See Hans-Josef Klauck, *1. Korintherbrief* (Würzburg, Germany: Echter Verlag, 1987), 25.
69. Through God's intrusion into reality, man's horizon of understanding is subjected to a reevaluation that will deconstruct man's expectation of how the Messiah / Christ or the arrival of divine wisdom will become evident. See Helmut Merklein, *Der erste Brief an die Korinther*: 1, *Kapitel* 1–4 (Gütersloh, Germany: Gütersloher Mohn, 1992): "The language of the cross creates a semantic paradigm shift and demands a new understanding. This occurs through 'faith' (1 Cor 1:21) because it is futile to want to know God through the assistance of human wisdom. True 'knowledge' of God . . . only exists through acknowledging the semantic system established on the cross" (174).

we proclaim Christ crucified, a stumbling block to Jews and foolishness to Gentiles, but to those who are the called, both Jews and Greeks, Christ the power of God and the wisdom of God. For God's foolishness is wiser than human wisdom, and God's weakness is stronger than human strength" (1 Cor 1:23–25).

In a positive interpretation, the event of the cross can be viewed in a way that specifically emphasizes God's divinity; the event of redemption doesn't merely exceed man's horizon of expectation but rather shatters it so that the event appears as something "unbelievable." In contrast, in a negative interpretation, God's intervention into human reality, in which man's horizon of expectation isn't crossed and remains totally within the framework of what he imagines God's divinity to be, would be simply and ultimately banal. God would prefer to solidify man's idolatrous perspective toward himself rather than secure, due to his greatness, an attitude of deference and respect from man.[70]

It is also clear that God's direct entrance into man's everyday world through his self-revelation didn't conform to the expectations of men of that time. The Christmas story in the Gospel of Luke (Luke 2:1–20) presents an astonishing contrast between the usual expectations of the arrival of the Messiah as well as the Roman emperor Augustus's supposed grip on power and the initial works of the Savior and Messiah once he has arrived (Luke 2:11).[71] If one examines more carefully the semantic content of the narrative account of the birth of Jesus, it becomes clear that it is not an attempt to offer a historic-naturalistic rendition; to the contrary, the narrative is very consciously shaped by the function of the Annunciation.[72] This is precisely why topoi that possess semantically ideological meanings are used and function in contrasting—that is, ironic—ways.

70. This explains why Alain Badiou detects the perspective of a ruler in both the Jewish and the Greek points of view. Alain Badiou, *Saint Paul: The Foundation of Universalism*, trans. Ray Bassier (Stanford, CA: Stanford University Press, 2003):

> Paul's profound idea is that Jewish discourse and Greek discourse are the two aspects of the same figure of mastery. . . . In the eyes of Paul the Jew, the weakness of Jewish discourse is that its logic of the exceptional sign is only valid *for* the Greek cosmic totality. The Jew is an exception to the Greek . . . and secondly, that the two discourses share the presupposition that the key to salvation is given to us within the universe, whether it be through direct mastery of the totality (Greek wisdom), or through mastery of a literal tradition and the deciphering of signs (Jewish ritualism and prophetism). (42)

71. See Jakob Kremer, *Lukasevangelium* (Würzburg, Germany: Echter Verlag, 1988), 36.
72. See Kremer, 38.

In the description of the birth of Jesus, the shepherds, as exemplary figures representing the poor,[73] proclaim the appearance of the "Savior" (Luke 2:11). The sovereign's title "Savior" isn't placed in a semantically indeterminate location but is rather a classical attribute for God (1 Sam 10:19; Bar 4:22; Exod 15:2; Isa 43:3, 11, et al.) and even for the Roman emperor. Other identifiers such as Lord (κύριος) and Messiah/Christ (χρῑστός) leave no doubt that another person in the contemporary world, perhaps the Roman emperor Augustus, could be the figure of the Savior of the world.[74] The irony of the narrative account, in which the figure of the Savior of the world is placed in a manger (Luke 2:7) rather than in a well-cushioned crib in an opulent sovereign's palace, is reinforced when the verb for proclamation—*εὐαγγελίζειν* (equivalent to the noun for good news, *εὐαγγέλιον*)—is used to describe the annunciation of the angel. At that time, the semantic field of this word—that is, of this group of words—is primarily located in the field of politics; in addition to its literal meaning, it would be used for the announcement of good news, preferably focused on the ideology of the Roman emperor.[75]

Using ideological language that is typical of a Roman emperor, especially for events like the birth of an heir apparent, the gospel declares the beginning of a new age. It is exactly at this point that the early Christians begin to create their own terminology: even Paul picks up on this and emphasizes the ironic-salutary dimension of the gospel of Jesus Christ, and even Mark uses this concept as a titular battle cry in order to juxtapose his description of the life of Jesus with those of the lives of the emperors of late antiquity.[76] If one accepts the two-source hypothesis that the Gospel of Mark was composed prior to Matthew and that Matthew and Luke depend on Mark, one can conclude with great confidence that "Jesus is supposed to be identified as the opposition ruler to Roman imperial power"[77] in Matthew and Luke and that his birth introduces a new era, the kingdom of God. The contrast between the overpowering Roman emperor and the needy child without a roof over his head could scarcely be portrayed more effectively: "The powerless Jesus of Nazareth, in contrast to Augustus and Jewish images of the Messiah, is the Savior and Bearer of Peace."[78]

73. See Josef Zmijewski, "Hirt. II. Neues Testament," in *LThK*, vol. 5, col. 155.
74. See Kremer, *Lukasevangelium*, 37.
75. See Martin Ebner, "B. III. Evangelium," in *Einleitung in das Neue Testament*, ed. Martin Ebner and Stefan Schreiber (Stuttgart, Germany: Kohlhammer, 2008), 117.
76. See Ebner, 118.
77. See Ebner, 120–21.
78. Kremer, *Lukasevangelium*, 39.

If one recognizes these semantically laden catchphrases and then examines the supposed intention of the text within the possible horizon of discourse, an ideological critique emerges that is not to be underestimated in which God's greatness, in its rational excess, offers a corrective to man's overhasty answers.

If one takes into account what has been presented so far, it is clear that the gospels are not meant to present a historic-naturalistic depiction of the life, work, suffering, and resurrection of Jesus Christ because each author of a gospel has his own intentions, within his own hermeneutic horizon, that are on an equal footing with his inspiration by the Holy Spirit. This surely explains why the four different gospels all proclaim the one gospel of Jesus Christ, but each one has its own subjectively conditioned emphasis. Therefore, Vatican II, in DV 11 (975–76), is obligated to (1) avoid creating conflict in regard to the relationship of pneumatologically motivated inspiration and the writings of humans and (2) avoid degrading biblical authors by referring to them as mere "writing instruments" (instrumenta ad scribendum)[79] or as "secretaries"[80] who transcribed whatever was dictated to them by the Holy Spirit (Spiritus Sancto dictante).[81] The exact proportions of the divine and human contributions and the exact mechanics of inspiration are deliberately left open and undefined.[82] The fact that the same attribute "auctor" is ascribed to both God as well as the biblical authors indicates that they both are on the same level and should be viewed as equal partners in the composition of the biblical text:

> Those things revealed by God which are contained and presented in the text of Holy Scripture were written under the influence of the Holy Spirit. By the faith handed down from the apostles, holy mother church accepts as sacred and canonical all the books of both the old Testament and the new, in their entirety and with all their parts, in the conviction that they were written under the inspiration of the holy Spirit (see Jn 20:31; 2 Tim 3:16; 2 Pet 1:19–21; 3:15–16) and therefore have God as their originator: on this basis they were handed on to the church. In the process of composition of the sacred books God chose and employed human agents, using their

79. DH, 3293.
80. DH, 3292.
81. See Helmut Hoping, "Theologischer Kommentar zur Dogmatischen Konstitution über die göttliche Offenbarung, *Dei verbum*," in HThK, vol. 3, 766.
82. See Hoping, 767.

> own powers and faculties, in such a way that they wrote as authors in the true sense, and yet God acted in and through them, directing the content entirely and solely as he willed.[83]

As is clear from the council text, Norman P. Tanner supports translating the Latin text such that the Latin word *auctores* doesn't mean "author" but rather, in keeping with the general gist of the passage, is translated in the sense of "originator" and "writer." This should be viewed favorably because it rejects the possible claim that one of the two sides—divine or human—would have authority over the language, the semantic meaning of its contents, the horizon of reception, or the text in general. This sovereignty would then allow for two extremes: As soon as man was considered the true "author" of the biblical text, he would have power over statements about God and man's experiences with God. Statements about God's being would then necessarily have to present God's essence and existence in a manner that would no longer allow for any distinction between God and the biblical text. A christological interpretation of Proverbs 8:22–34 would no longer be possible because the description of creation would have been considered a direct, realistic representation of reality; this would make any hermeneutic interpretation impossible that allowed for change in one's respective horizon of understanding. Likewise, the apparent contradiction between Isaiah 45:7 and 1 John 4:8 and 4:16 wouldn't refer to God's inexpressible greatness, and even the various intentions and traditions of statements in the Gospel of Matthew such as Matthew 24:45–51 and Matthew 11:28–30 would suddenly be on the same level. To be blunt, if the biblical author had absolute authority over the text, based on his sovereignty, God would then become a pawn of the author and his words. In turn, direct sovereignty on God's part would lead to difficulties as well. If God himself had determined every single word in the Bible, it would lead, to a certain extent, to the *inlibration* of God into Holy Scripture; this would mean, first of all, that there would no longer be any difference between God, with his will for salvation, and the text itself because his will for salvation would be directly portrayed in the Bible. Furthermore, there wouldn't have been any human freedom in the final editing process of the Bible because the text would have been received as

83. DV 11, 975–76.

a divinely inspired, word-for-word transmission. Man would be God's writing instrument, and lacking *ratio*, he would neither have his own intentionality nor be embedded in a historical-hermeneutic discourse. There would be no human freedom in the writing process due to the force of God's will.[84]

The other extreme—attributing full authorship to man—would have placed the faithful in a position of sovereignty because man would have had access to God's will. The faithful would be in a position superior to all other human beings because their direct access to God's will would give them interpretive authority over the world. They would possess esoteric knowledge and therefore be in a position of power over the ignorant.[85] The extent of their potential for power is evident without further explanation; despite the dangers, it needn't be further discussed at this point because there is no ambiguity.

The fact that the early church had already taken a position against the identical depiction of the event of salvation in a *single* interpretive horizon based on its absolute correctness is evident in its dealings with Marcion's understanding of the canon. Marcion based his canon solely on the Gospel of Luke and a selection of ten Epistles of Paul, and he rejected the writings of the Hebrew Bible (the Old Testament), the remaining three gospels, and the other Epistles of the New Testament. From this possibly gnostic horizon, Marcion declares that the Old Testament, with its (Jewish) Creator God, is outdated and has been superseded, whereas the New Testament (Gospel of Luke and ten Epistles of Paul), with Jesus's proclamation of God the Redeemer, is the new guiding principle (Greek: κανών, "standard, guiding principle") for an understanding of the world.[86] The early Church Fathers proposed an understanding of the canon that differed from Marcion's interpretative authority in regard to his dismissal of the Old Testament because of his binary distinction between old-traditional-incorrect and new-authoritative-correct. This alternative

84. If a person considers such a perspective to be acceptable and comprehensible—claiming that sacred Scripture would otherwise be lacking dignity and sanctity—this person is being led down a slippery slope that can very quickly change from Biblicism to fundamentalism. This kind of literal reading of God's will actually makes human reflection on the correctness of what is written unnecessary—that is, to a great extent, it discourages it. From this perspective, one can only go to war with the Bible.
85. See Michel Foucault, *Discipline and Punish: The Birth of the Prison*, trans. Alan Sheridan (New York: Vintage, 1979), 27–31.
86. See Martin Ebner, "A. 1. Der christliche Kanon," in Ebner and Schreiber, *Einleitung in das Neue Testament*, 25–28.

canon of the church can be summarized in three points: plurality, complementarity, and the Jewish foundation of faith.[87]

Rather than accepting Marcion's narrow view that the event of salvation was presented *correctly* in only one gospel, the Church Fathers addressed the plurality and thus also the complementarity of the four gospels; this revealed that none of them alone directly depicts the *one* gospel of Jesus Christ but rather that each one bears witness to a historical situation from a perspective of faith. Although selecting canonical texts always results in the exclusion of some texts, this process of canonizing the Bible shows that the focus wasn't on simplistic correctness but rather on making it possible to tie together an orthodox panorama of perspectives. Inconsistencies and supposed contradictions are taken seriously as perspectival peculiarities and aren't erased due to a grand wish for harmonization. In addition, texts like the *Diatessaron*, Tatian's attempt to harmonize the four gospels, are rejected. Tatian's interpretive authority can be seen in his elimination of contradictions and inconsistencies or their integration into the larger framework of the Gospel of John in such a way that they no longer exist. His purpose was simply to declare the following: there should be a single, unambiguous statement of the gospels. Hence Christianity's message no longer recognizes any narrative contradictions because the problematic points have been erased. However, it's problematic that Tatian's gospel harmony, despite the enormous gap in time—it was composed around 180 CE—could alone decide which account of the life, suffering, and resurrection of Jesus Christ is the correct one.[88] Of course, the product of this man's interpretive authority was then attacked and replaced by a compilation of the four gospels, albeit with some delay and despite the broad distribution of this gospel harmony.[89]

God's intervention into human reality therefore gives rise to increased pressure to distinguish between the incarnation of the Word and the witnesses of this incarnation and the subsequent acts, suffering, death, and resurrection. There are fundamental qualitative differences between the divine Word and man's bearing witness to this event in human speech: "The Word is not said in any tongue, since he transgresses language itself, seeing that, Word in flesh and bone, he is given

87. See Ebner, 30.
88. See Ebner, 28–30.
89. See Ebner, 29.

as indissolubly speaker, sign, and referent. . . . Incarnate in our words, the Word acquires in them a new unspeakableness, since he can be spoken in them only by the movement of incarnation that is, so to speak, anterior to the words, which he speaks and which he lets speak him."[90]

Nevertheless, one should encounter the biblical text with deference and respect because its normativity derives from the fact that it was written "under the inspiration of the holy Spirit" (DV 11, 975). This constitutes the normativity of the faithful of the church.[91] From this perspective, and in the context of faith, the biblical text can become an icon of God. This emphasizes the fundamental difference between God and the biblical text. God is not the Bible:

> For it is not a question here first of a thought, but of a referent, in flesh and bone, of the Word whose incarnation occupies and transgresses at once the order of speech and of meaning. No human tongue can say the Said of ~~God~~. For to say it, one must speak as He alone speaks, with *exousia* (Mark 1:22, etc.), with that sovereign freedom, whose (super-) natural ascendency impresses all as an omnipotence so great that it only has to speak in order to be admitted. The Word says itself, it therefore becomes unspeakable to us; labile inhabitant of our babble, it inhabits our babble nevertheless as referent.[92]

God himself takes the initiative, and it was his intent to appear to man and reveal himself (DV 2, 972). This is foundational; it makes it possible for believers to take a second step through God's self-revelation and to bear witness, through access to the Holy Spirit, in their own words and within their own hermeneutic horizon (DV 12, 976). The perspective that God became incarnate in the world through Jesus Christ is only accessible through faith because one couldn't determine from Christ's pure humanity (Menschsein) in a rational way that he is the second person in the inner-Trinitarian event of redemption; therefore, in the Gospel of

90. Marion, *God*, 141.
91. See Hoping, "Kommentar," 766.
92. Marion, *God*, 142.

John, the answer to the disciples' question about the visible accessibility to God is as follows:[93]

> Philip said to him, "Lord, show us the Father, and we will be satisfied." Jesus said to him, "Have I been with you all this time, Philip, and you still do not know me? Whoever has seen me has seen the Father. How can you say, 'Show us the Father'? Do you not believe that I am in the Father and the Father is in me? The words that I say to you I do not speak on my own; but the Father who dwells in me does his works. Believe me that I am in the Father and the Father is in me; but if you do not, then believe me because of the works themselves." (John 14:8–11)

Thus it is fitting to interpret iconically the perspective of looking at the Father through Jesus Christ so that the Pauline view can also be connected to Christ (Col 1:15: "He is the image of the invisible God, the firstborn of all creation"). God's transcendence continues to be guaranteed (Exod 33:20), and Jesus Christ is nevertheless granted a position of prior existence—that is, he was preexistent to creation.[94] The Absolute—that is, that which is always invisible—continues to remain invisible even when God intrudes into human reality. A stance of openness toward faith in

93. Therefore, through Christ's incarnation, the Absolute continues to be only indirectly discernible; this removes any sense of force that God's direct presence in man's horizon would create. The transition—that Jesus Christ's presence in human form makes indirect access to the Father through faith possible—can be connected to Lyotard's (and therefore Derrida's) reflections on the Absolute. The Absolute only appears indirectly, as a trace of absence. See Wendel, "Nichtsprechendes Sprechen":

> In order for the Absolute to appear, in order for its "arrival" to even happen, it must be able to appear—if not directly, then indirectly. However, this kind of indirect presentation, in any case, can only be the presence of absence, the portrayal of the non-portrayable of the Absolute. This can, however, be described as a negative portrayal, because the portrayal doesn't represent a presence and therefore doesn't represent something that hasn't been portrayed, a lack of an object, but rather only a formal, empty absence and unportrayability. This negative portrayal of the Absolute is carried out as a trace, as a sign: "For Ideas, there are no presentable objects—there are only *analoga*, signs, hypotyposes." In this context, trace, mark, or symbol don't mean a likeness of an original image because the Absolute isn't an essence, a Being (Seiendes), or a concealed content; to the contrary, it is withdrawal, concealment, absence itself, that eludes identification. (273–74)

(Translator's note: The source of the internal quote is Jean-François Lyotard, *The Postmodern Explained: Correspondence* 1982–1985, ed. Julian Pefanis and Morgan Thomas, trans. Don Barry et al. [Minneapolis: University of Minnesota Press, 1993], 70.)

94. See Josef Pfammater, *Epheserbrief: Kolosserbrief* (Würzburg, Germany: Echter Verlag, 1987), 61–62.

which man doesn't even attempt to want to define God makes it then possible for God to prove his divinity, even beyond human life (Dasein) in its rational form.[95]

God's greatness, which is situated beyond all temporal or other limiting dimensions, therefore transcends the biblical text by necessity, but it doesn't in any way diminish its inspirational dignity and sacredness without any flaws. Through the influence of the Holy Spirit, the Bible is and remains the sacred text of the church.

The Human Horizon and the Intrusion of Absolute Reality

The intrusion of the divine—whether it be when God shows his divinity by revealing his name in the Exodus event or through God's incarnation, which culminates in the overcoming of human mortality through the resurrection—greatly disturbs man and his usual orientation toward the world. Man's horizon of expectation is incompatible with his lived experience when he encounters God:

> In clear contrast to this Jewish-Christian notion of truth as relying on an external traumatic encounter (the divine Call to the Jewish people, God's call to Abraham, the inscrutable Grace—all totally incompatible with our inherent qualities, even with our innate ethics), both paganism and Gnosticism (the reinscription of the Jewish-Christian stance back into paganism) conceive the path to truth as the "inner journey" of spiritual self-purification, as the return to one's true Inner Self, the self's "rediscovery." Kierkegaard was right when he pointed out that the central opposition in Western spirituality is between Socrates and Christ: the inner journey of remembrance versus rebirth through the shock of the external encounter. Within the Jewish-Christian field, God Himself is the ultimate harasser, the intruder who brutally disturbs the harmony of our lives.[96]

This raises the question of how man is to deal with God's intrusion into his reality or if he can even deal with it at all because, on the one hand, reality and God's

95. See Marion, *God*, 63.
96. Slavoj Žižek, *How to Read Lacan* (New York: W. W. Norton, 2006), 99. See also Slavoj Žižek, *Event: A Philosophical Journey through a Concept* (Brooklyn: Melvin House, 2014), 35.

being are closed off to him—that is, are unknowable—whereas, on the other hand, through God's self-revelation and his name, man is in a position to make statements from his horizon.

Jacques Lacan's epistemological perspective on human reality offers a methodological approach for exploring these questions.[97] He developed a triadic model for the structure of man's horizon of reality, consisting of the Symbolic, the Imaginary, and the Real.[98] To be sure, these categories can be distinguished from one another in a theoretical analysis based on their essence, but as representations of the interlinking of reality, they create a Borromean knot. This model is composed of three parts that are entirely interdependent on one another; otherwise, the structure falls apart.[99] The Symbolic is the most important category for Lacanian theory because the analyst can begin here. The Symbolic has its own dual structure that, by necessity, requires something additional if it is to really exist; in this regard, the Symbolic is similar to language. There is the signifier (name, sign, form) and the signified (meaning, content, being). Signifiers are part of man's lived experience because they build the basic framework for human understanding. They are the prereflexive network of man's lived experience, where he finds order, structure, and therefore also the law.[100] The signified, the semantic content, has to be differentiated from the signifiers. The signified is not tied, by necessity, to signifiers; in fact, it is produced through subjective connection and gets connected to them.[101] According to Lacan, it must become clear in analytic observation "that the signified has nothing to do with the ears, but only with reading—the reading of the signifiers we hear. The signified is not what

97. Questions regarding faith in God are not being thematicized and psychoanalytically evaluated from an atheistic point of view in this investigation. It is axiomatic for this investigation that one accepts the true reality of God, who revealed himself through Jesus Christ. Whether the belief in God is a collective obsessive-compulsive disorder is a topic for Freudian psychoanalysis but not for doctrinal theology.

98. See Jacques Lacan, *Encore: The Seminar of Jacques Lacan*, bk. 20, 1972–1973: *On Feminine Sexuality: The Limits of Love and Knowledge*, ed. Jacques-Alain Miller, trans. Bruce Fink (New York: W. W. Norton, 1999), 90.

99. See Lacan, 123–24. See also Žižek, *Lacan*, 8; and likewise, Evans, *Dictionary*, 18–20.

100. See Jacques Lacan, *The Four Fundamental Concepts of Psychoanalysis: The Seminar of Jacques Lacan*, bk. 11, ed. Jacques-Alain Miller, trans. Alan Sheridan (New York: W. W. Norton, 1998), 20, 44–45. See also Lacan, *Psychoses*, 183–85. According to Lacan, this chain or network of signifiers that are all interconnected to one another and mutually dependent in their synchronicity—without having a firm, semantic core—has had a significant influence on the hermeneutic, philosophical theories of structuralism, poststructuralism, and deconstruction. See Benedikt Jeßing and Ralph Köhnen, *Einführung in die Neuere deutsche Literaturwissenschaft* (Stuttgart, Germany: J. B. Metzler, 2007), 305–18.

101. See Lacan, *Four Fundamental Concepts*, 211–12; see Lacan, *Encore*, 29; see also Evans, *Dictionary*, 185–87.

you hear. What you hear is the signifier. The signified is the effect of the signifier."[102] Language and speech only take place in social interaction; signifying chains, as well as their semantic content, therefore need a counterpart to open up their structure and meaning. To a certain extent, speech functions as an exchange of symbols that is located beyond technical instrumentalization.[103] Signifiers and signified are separated from one another, but this gap between both elements of the sign is forgotten and remains unconscious in daily interactions.[104] In order for this random network of signifiers to have a fixed point that binds them together, it needs an empty signifier: *the big Other.*

This is the subjectivized order that generally grants space so that the signifying chains of signifiers—that is, the network of symbols—have ample space;[105] this allows the big Other to become connected to the master signifier. The master signifier is at the end of a signifying chain because it exists without a signified and is therefore the basis providing structure, but it is also indestructible because it isn't deconstructable.[106] Lacan transitions from his readings of Freud about the totally prohibitive father—*Totem and Taboo*, among other works. In order to ensure that the incest taboo can gain far-reaching validity, he dissolves this very strict coupling of prohibition and the person of the father and then merges the prohibition with the Name-of-the-Father (i.e., the father metaphor).[107] The Name-of-the-Father thereby becomes the foundation of the symbolic-legitimate order—the Name-of-the-Father (as an empty signifier) is the law itself:[108] "It is in the *name of the father* that we must recognize the basis of the symbolic function which, since

102. Lacan, *Encore*, 33. Man himself creates a further reality, beyond animalistic reality, through the meanings that have been generated. Man fills his predetermined network of signifiers with (more or less) fictitious meanings—this is how man creates meaning in existence (Sein). See Lacan, *On the Names-of-the-Father*, trans. Bruce Fink (Malden, MA: Polity, 2013), 44–45.
103. See Lacan, *Écrits*, 75–81, 95–96, 108, 225. Symbolically structured interaction is essential to every social order; society can't exist without it. See also Lacan: "Man thus speaks, but it is because the symbol has made him man. Even if, in fact, overabundant gifts welcome a stranger who has made himself known to a group, the life of natural groups that constitute a community is subject to the rules of matrimonial alliance—determining the direction in which the exchange of women takes place—and to the mutual services determined by marriage. . . . Marriage ties are governed by an order of preference whose law concerning kinship names is, like language, imperative for the group in its forms, but unconscious in its structure" (229).
104. See Lacan, 229.
105. See Lacan, *Psychoses*, 36–40; and Žižek, *Lacan*, 40–42.
106. See Lacan, *Psychoses*, 184.
107. See Lacan, *Names-of-the-Father*, 74; and Lacan, *Écrits*, 481–89.
108. Lacan himself recognized that this process is similar to God's revelation of his name to Moses at Mount Sinai, where God discloses that his revealed name is a purely fundamental signifier that says nothing other than the name itself. See Lacan, *Names-of-the-Father*, 79.

the dawn of historical time, has identified his person with the figure of the law."[109] If the Name-of-the-Father is lacking or even rejected, the network of the symbolic order will collapse, along with the structural network of signifiers because the fixed point of the structure has disappeared:[110]

> The symbolic father is the *Name-of-the-Father*. He is the essentially communicative element of the symbolic world and its structure. It is necessary for that weaning, that is more essential than the first weaning in which the child emerges from its plain and simple bond with its maternal almighty one. The *Name-of-the-Father* is essential to every expression of human speech; this is the reason why it is written in *Ecclesiastes* that "*Foolishness spoke in his heart: There is no God.*"
>
> Why does he say "in his heart?" Because he can't say in his mouth.[111]

Interpreted in a positive light, the Name-of-the-Father is the guarantor of the symbolic order; in contrast, the prohibition isn't only limited to the person of the father but extends beyond the individual and attains universal validity.[112] But something else is also happening here: to a certain extent, this is also an overcoming through an encounter with the Real power of the person of the father who has intruded from outside. The power of this real person, who won't let himself be controlled by man, is banished to the Symbolic, where, on the one hand, this power can be controlled by man, at least to a certain extent, but on the other hand, due to its limitations, it becomes universalized.[113]

109. Lacan, *Écrits*, 230. In his early writings, Lacan writes the name of the father (*nom du père*) in small letters without hyphens. Over the course of his work, this term becomes more important and achieves the status of a well-defined (working) concept that is now capitalized and hyphenated (Nom-du-Père). See also Evans, *Dictionary*, 119. For simplicity's sake, with the exception of citations from Lacan's early writings, "Name-of-the-Father" will be written as its own term with hyphens.
110. See Lacan, *Écrits*, 481–82.
111. Jacques Lacan, *Die Objektbeziehung*, *Das Seminar Buch* IV (1956–57), ed. Jacques-Alain Miller, trans. (from French) Hans-Dieter Gondek (Vienna: Turia + Kant, 2003), 428. (Translator's note: There is currently no published version of this text in English. Translated passages from the German edition into English are my own.)
112. See Žižek, *Ticklish Subject*: Žižek writes that "the murder of the father is an event which had to take place in reality" (315).
113. See Slavoj Žižek, *The Fragile Absolute: Or, Why Is the Christian Legacy Worth Fighting For?* (London: Verso, 2001), 75. Only through the symbolic father (as the Name-of-the-Father) can the structure of the law produce a social, universal, and thereby communicative order: "What is missing is the father as the bearer of symbolic authority, the Name-of-the-Father, the prohibitory 'castrating' agency that enables the subject's entry into the symbolic order, and thus into the domain of *desire*. The two fathers, imaginary and real, are what is left over once paternal symbolic authority disintegrates" (75).

Following Lacan, this analysis sees a close correlation between the Symbolic and language. Nevertheless, the Symbolic must not be equated with language itself; they are not identical. Language possesses, besides its share in the Symbolic, a large share in the Imaginary (the second order of the Borromean knot). Man is not a static being; from the very beginning, man is in the mirror stage. This means that man recognizes (consciously or unconsciously/prereflexively) his own current position and attempts to approximate it to an imaginary—in part, illusory—image and to recreate himself, from this situation, into this imaginary "I."[114] In later deliberations, Lacan integrates the Imaginary into the triadic order of the Borromean knot and expands his earlier thoughts by locating the source of the Imaginary in man's (self-) alienation.[115] Man would like to come into his own—that is, he wants to gain self-confidence and self-assurance—by being acknowledged by others.[116] The root of human desire lies here, in a narcissistic dimension, where narcissism itself is still able to be differentiated from desire.[117] Man is in a situation of self-alienation and imagines a likeness of how he wants to be—that is, how he should be; this image is called the ideal ego.[118] Man imagines, in an illusory way, that there will be a successful synthesis of the current stage of his ego and a final, idealized stage of his ego in the future.[119] In summary, one can say that the Imaginary possesses a dual structure in which a current structure is aligned with an ideal structure that has yet to be realized.[120] The Imaginary is man's consistent standard for measuring his own reality and determining whether his reality corresponds to what it should be.[121]

The Real, the third order of the Borromean knot, is surely the part of Lacan's psychoanalytic theory that is of greatest interest to theology. This concept pervades Lacan's entire work and frequently presents new connotations and considerations—that is, shifts in meaning—that may not be indicated in other

114. See Lacan, *Écrits*, 75–81.
115. See Lacan, *Psychoses*: "Alienation is constitutive of the imaginary order. Alienation is the imaginary as such" (146).
116. See Lacan, *Écrits*: "In short, nowhere does it appear more clearly that man's desire finds its meaning in the other's desire, not so much because the other holds the keys to the desired object, as because his first object(ive) is to be recognized by the other" (222).
117. See Evans, *Dictionary*, 82–84.
118. See Žižek, *Lacan*, 80.
119. See Evans, *Dictionary*, 52.
120. See Evans, 84–85.
121. In order for man to overcome his illusory self-deception, he has to acknowledge and overcome his self-alienation. See Lacan, *Names-of-the-Father*: "The ego is something in which the subject cannot recognize himself at first except by alienating himself. He can thus only refind himself by abolishing the ego's *alter ego*" (24). Man has to transgress his own phantasms.

works.[122] Instead of viewing these shifts in the meaning of the Real as a negative, they reflect the precision of this concept; it can't be defined per se because the Real itself can't be defined.[123] Slavoj Žižek writes the following about the Real: "What all this amounts to is that for Lacan the Real, at its most radical, has to be totally de-substantialized. It is not an external thing that resists being caught in the symbolic network, but the fissure within the symbolic network itself."[124]

Even though Žižek states that it is a (simplistic) temptation to translate Lacan's Real into a notion of God,[125] this perspective is not meant to do violence to Lacan's concept of the Real; it is envisioned by Lacan himself.[126] God is a reality that intrudes from outside and can't be grasped by our man-made system of symbols; this presents a continually irritating encounter for man. Meeting the Real becomes an unsettling encounter for man. It is a traumatic meeting, and its tension can't be fully defused through a symbolic ordering.[127] Here man encounters the Real through anxiety.

The encounter between the Israelites and their God is not that different. To the contrary, one can use the vocabulary of psychoanalysis to describe the encounter with the Real that is narrated in Exodus 3:14–16, as Žižek does when he writes "that a God is encountered in the real. As every real is inaccessible, it is signaled by what does not mislead: anxiety."[128] This encounter with the Real is traumatic for man; Old Testament theology uses powerful imagery in these passages to show how heavily laden with meaning this encounter is. In the dialogue between God and Moses, God warns him not to want to look directly at him: "'But,' he said, 'you cannot see my face; for no one shall see me and live'" (Exod 33:20).

122. See Evans, *Dictionary*, 159–61.
123. The Real is not to be confused with reality. Reality is the symbolic order in which man moves and where he can find his way. The Real is realer than reality because the Real always stands in man's way and is inaccessible and uncategorizable.
124. Žižek, *Lacan*, 72.
125. See Žižek, 72.
126. Lacan himself does not want to go to bat for theism. To the contrary, he distances himself from a theistic interpretation of reality, albeit without seeking to destroy theism through a militant gesture. See Lacan, *Die Objektbeziehung*, 428.
127. See Lacan, *Four Fundamental Concepts*, 67–70. This encounter with the Real shows the division that permeates all of reality: man's division/alienation between the ego and the ideal ego in the Imaginary, as well as the division between the signifier and the signified in the Symbolic—this is where the foundation through the Symbolic-Real occurs (the Name-of-the-Father, the big Other, etc.)—illustrate the idea of the Borromean knot in its inseparability. The parts of the knot are always interdependent and interlinked so that no part can exist without other parts. In order for the Real to be experienced as the Real, there needs to be a symbolic order that can be crossed. Without the Name-of-the-Father, the Father remains unrecognizable in his Father-Being (Vater-Sein). See Žižek, *Ticklish Subject*, 102; see also Slavoj Žižek, *On Belief* (New York: Routledge, 2001), 85–88.
128. Lacan, *Names-of-the-Father*, 80.

Man's horizon of interpretation (the Symbolic) is not in a position to integrate the intrusion of the Real—that is, of the Absolute—in such a way that he could reconstruct it into a consistent, coherent system. Through the intervention of the Real, man is confronted by a quality of incomprehensibility; Lacan therefore presents the Real to man as the "impossible." This "impossible" has to be more than a static concept of substance because substance already plays a central role in human logic and can be classified as a category.[129] One can easily make a transition from this idea to the writings of Jean-Luc Marion without having to make significant reinterpretations. The main purpose of Marion's methodological correction to the concept of God is to relocate God beyond what is comprehensible to humans—that is, earthly creatures. God is beyond substance, beyond Being (Sein).[130] God's divinity is proven because it (1) is communicated and offered to man through the event of revelation and (2) can never be sufficiently accessed within man's horizons of concepts and understanding.[131]

An intrusion of the Real into man's reality is unpredictable, uncontrollable, and above all, incomprehensible.[132] For man, it is "originally unwelcome"[133] because it is uncontrollable. It is a traumatic experience for man.[134] The encounter with the Real is a classic, religious situation within the Judeo-Christian horizon; this explains why Lacan introduces Abraham and Søren Kierkegaard into his discussion of the Real.[135]

This encounter with God raises the question of man himself because his entire understanding of reality is put into question. Truth is not something that can be recollected from within as is suggested in Socratic-Platonic philosophy; rather, it intrudes incomprehensibly from outside and forces man to take a stance—acceptance or rejection—toward the Absolute and the truth: "The Christian Truth, in contrast, is the one of Revelation, which is the exact opposite of reminiscence: Truth is not inherent, it is not the (re)discovery of what is already in myself, but an Event, something violently *imposed* on me from the Outside through a traumatic encounter that shatters the very foundations of my being."[136]

129. See Žižek, *Lacan*, 72.
130. See Marion, *God*, 44–45, 15.
131. See Marion, 61–66.
132. See Lacan, *Four Fundamental Concepts*, 53–54, 68–70.
133. Lacan, 69.
134. See Žižek, *On Belief*, 86–87.
135. See Lacan, *Names-of-the-Father*, 78–88.
136. Žižek, *Ticklish Subject*, 212.

Žižek writes that the plausibility of belief in God is only a secondary phase in man's world horizon. Man doesn't search for reasons and proofs that will lend support to the plausibility of his belief in God until after he has made the leap of faith and determined the validity of God's intrusion.[137] Nevertheless, these reasons do not allow one to present the validity of one's own faith in a manner that is universally valid and that would make this position both plausible and reasonable in a compelling way to a counterpart, who is beyond the position of faith and has neither recognized nor experienced the idea of the Real—that is, of God. According to Žižek, one doesn't become a believer through reason; relying on Lacan's Real and Kierkegaard's radical subjectivity, he writes the following: "The notion of belief . . . was elaborated by Kierkegaard; this is why, for him, *religion is eminently modern*: the traditional universe is ethical, while the Religious involves a radical disruption of the Old Ways—true religion is a crazy wager on the Impossible we have to make."[138]

Faith can be viewed as an existential acceptance after an encounter with the incomprehensible, with the unsymbolizable Real[139]—that is, the Absolute—in which this stance of acceptance can't be articulated in a manner that makes it universally comprehensible and thereby logically *persuasive*.

Kierkegaard communicates this by using the pseudonym Johannes de Silentio.[140] Johannes expresses his high regard for Abraham but states repeatedly that Abraham's actions toward his fellow men and above all to Isaac, although based

137. See Žižek, *Lacan*, 29. See also Žižek, *Event*, 4, 132–33. Jürgen Bründl makes a similar point when he confirms the constant "Too Late" of theology in its ongoing argumentation and reflection. Because Christian theology is only possible from the perspective of faith, there can be no theology before the act of faith. See Jürgen Bründl, *Gottes Nähe: Der Heilige Geist und das Problem der Negativität in der Theologie* (Freiburg, Germany: Herder, 2010): "As a consequence, theological thought becomes a rethinking of a special kind; it has an *a posteriori* character and therefore leads to the untenable position of having to have understood something about which, at the outset, there is nothing rational to be said, to the extent that it is humanly possible" (11).

138. Žižek, *Ticklish Subject*, 115.

139. Even though Lacan's concept of the Real comes close to God's incomprehensibility, it ought to be mentioned that even this term is an ever-failing attempt to conceptualize what is beyond humans' capability. Relating to Lacan's conception in an appropriate way, the Judeo-Christian God also holds parts of the Symbolic and the Imaginary. Therefore, God is not reducible to the Real, strictly speaking.

140. Kierkegaard's use of the pseudonym makes it clear that he isn't claiming to be the author. Whatever Kierkegaard himself can't say, and is even unsayable, can only be said, to some extent, through the fictitious character of Johannes de Silentio. He says the unsayable. See Konrad Paul Liessmann, *Sören Kierkegaard zur Einführung* (Hamburg, Germany: Junius, 2006): "As is always the case in Kierkegaard, the pseudonyms are meaningful. The name 'Johannes de Silentio,' i.e., *Johannes of Silence* . . . already suggests that what is actually of concern to him can't be expressed. His 'Dialectical Lyric,' the subtitle of *Fear and Trembling*, will side-step, circle around, and hint at the problem, but never name it. Johannes de Silentio presents . . . the circumstances under which the ethical can or must be suspended" (58).

on his faith and his clinging to God's promise, are incomprehensible. Johannes himself can't believe how Abraham, believing in God, trusts through the power of the absurd: "I cannot make the movement of faith. I cannot shut my eyes and plunge confidently into the absurd; it is for me an impossibility, but I do not praise myself for that."[141]

141. Søren Kierkegaard, *Fear and Trembling/Repetition*, ed. and trans. Howard V. Hong and Edna H. Hong (Princeton, NJ: Princeton University Press, 1983), 34.

3

Human Speech about God

The Perspective of the Faithful

Faith is a stage of being human (Menschsein) that can be neither compelled by arguments about its plausibility nor imposed upon man by an outside power. The condition of having faith is only possible through an invitation granted by God, and only God has divine sovereignty to make this invitation.[1] Augustine explains the possibility of inferring God's intentions and of recognizing his greatness so that God will accept man and bestow on him great inspiration (*illuminatio*) founded on grace, and this inspiration won't be subject to man's power or be accessible to him.[2] In the context of Augustine's *illuminatio*, faith is a receptive event that originates from God alone and therefore can't be communicated through some created third party (a teacher or a written statement). An *illuminatio*—a person who participates in and is inspired by divine wisdom through grace—comes in the form of a gift to man; this gift is offered to man but is not forced upon him in any way. Man's free will remains unchanged and intact because he can block God's devotion to him at any time.[3] However, this can lead to heresy and sin.[4]

1. The separation of the act of faith (*fides qua creditur*) and the contents of faith (*fides quae creditur*) is a classical distinction in fundamental theology. For simplicity's sake, English equivalents are used in this work.
2. See Augustine, *The Works of Saint Augustine: A Translation for the 21st Century*, ed. John E. Rotelle, trans. Maria Boulding, vol. 1/1, *The Confessions* (Hyde Park, NY: New City Press, 2015), 108. In Augustine's description of his own situation, he writes that it was impossible for him to be inspired—that is, to have access to God's mystery of salvation—based on his own strength and his own will. He had to rely on God turning toward him and illuminating his darkness. See also Frederick van Fleteren, "Illuminatio," in AL, vol. 3, col. 498.
3. See Volker Henning Drecoll, "Gratia," in AL, vol. 3, cols. 196, 200, 206–7. In regard to the phenomenon of nonbelievers and the question of why God only chose certain people, Augustine, following Romans 11:33 and Romans 9:14, points to God's unfathomable greatness. See also Augustine, "A Treatise on the Spirit and the Letter," in *Nicene and Post-Nicene Fathers*, 1st ser., ed. Philip Schaff, trans. Peter Holmes, Robert Ernest Wallis, and Benjamin Warfield (Peabody, MA: Hendrickson, 1994), 5:110.
4. See Fleteren, "Illuminatio," cols. 498–500.

Augustine attributes the fact that man can even become a believer entirely to God's initial gesture, his turning toward man. Thus the summons and the choice to be open to finding faith are closely tied to God's previous actions. This explains why Augustine introduces the concept of *praescientia* in the initial phase of his Paul exegesis; according to Paul, it wasn't Abraham's merit but his faith that led him to righteousness (Rom 4:1–5, 13). Because God's act of choice doesn't arise out of human actions but rather originates in man's faith, Augustine makes the point that there is a *praescientia* of God that neither repeals nor bypasses man's free will. God knows who will declare their faith to him and accept faith; he chooses these individuals.[5] Augustine turns away from the concept of *praescientia* and even rejects it in the course of the Pelagian and semi-Pelagian conflicts. He replaces it with *praedestinatio*, which he uses as a synonym:[6] "These gifts, therefore, of God, which are given to the elect who are called according to God's purpose, among which gifts is both the beginning of belief and perseverance in the faith to the termination of this life . . . these gifts of God, I say, if there is no predestination as I am maintaining, are not foreknown by God. But they are foreknown. This, therefore, is the predestination which I maintain."[7]

What is decisive—whether one uses the earlier term *praescientia* or the later term *praedestinatio*—is that the initial gesture originates from God and, at the outset, precedes man's act of faith. Before man decides to accept God's gift of faith, in an existential act, the possibility of man being able to believe was established and ordained through God's will for man's salvation. Man's ability to believe would not exist without God's will for salvation because man can neither mandate nor determine faith; he can only accept or reject it. This means that the paradoxes of man's justification of faith—that is, the purely rational, plausible grounds for faith—are always secondary to the act of faith itself. They can't be the motivation for the act of faith because faith is based on hope and therefore refers to a time in the future. Man trusts that God's promises will be fulfilled; this is the reason for

5. See Drecoll, "Gratia," col. 195. Augustine always speaks out on behalf of man's free will. This forms a distinctive part of his teaching; he continues to do this even when it isn't perfectly aligned with the rest of his theory of grace. It forms one of the two fixed points of the Augustinian theory of grace: (1) God's initial gesture toward man—unearned by man and inaccessible to him—to offer him grace and (2) man's free and willing acceptance of this invitation to grace.
6. See Drecoll, cols. 225–26.
7. Augustine, "A Treatise on the Gift of Perseverance," in Schaff, *Nicene and Post-Nicene Fathers*, 1st ser., 5:544.

faith. This trust isn't a blind suspension of one's understanding because *fides*—not only in the Augustinian sense[8]—is based on an individual who is trustworthy, who is worthy of trust, so that this individual can be trusted.[9] Alain Badiou likewise describes a profession of faith as speech in the future perfect verb tense because the content of the profession of faith has not yet been verified in the present. It is based on the belief that it is, on the one hand, already worthy of trust even though in regard to future promises, its status resides in the future. However, the believing subject is so convinced of the occurrence of this event—that is, of the truth that has been disclosed—that the believing subject speaks of the arrival of the truth in the future perfect tense.[10]

From Augustine's perspective, the devoutly personal act of trust culminates in one's trust in God at the event of Christ on the cross.[11] It follows from this that this most implausible event, which is total foolishness and absurdity, becomes believable through Jesus Christ. Through his death and resurrection at the event on the cross, Jesus Christ becomes the reason and the content of *fides* and therefore of faith. The devout Christian trusts that the salvation of the world lies in Christ's disgraceful martyrdom. He trusts that the Old Testament perspective of cursing the man who will be put to death on wood—that is, on a stake—will be transgressed (Deut 21:23) and that the world will be saved because God himself has accepted a cursed and disgraceful punishment (Gal 3:13–14). Yet this readiness to trust and this understanding are not directly granted to everyone; they depend on faith itself, which is God's gift of grace. Through his initial turning toward man, founded on grace, God invites such a person to accept this invitation to faith, to transgress the purely human perspective of foolishness, and to recognize the salvation of the world through Christ's death on the cross.

In the traditional understanding, the Holy Spirit takes charge of this openness to a new perspective toward the possibility of faith.[12] Johannine theology created the groundwork for this shift through the παράκλητος, a comforter and a guide who makes the incomprehensibility of the event of the cross understandable (John 16:7, 13). Based on these introductory remarks, one can claim that the Holy Spirit is the

8. See Eugene TeSelle, "Fides," in AL, vol. 2, cols. 1335–36.
9. See Agamben, *Sacrament*, 26–27.
10. See Badiou, *Being and Event*, 396–401.
11. See TeSelle, "Fides," col. 1335.
12. See Bründl, *Gottes Nähe*, 19, 51, 53.

hermeneutic necessity for insight into faith. However, faith is grace and the Holy Spirit doesn't merely have a functional role in the event of salvation. The Holy Spirit is the third person in a triune event and is worshipped with the same respect and dignity as the Father and the Son. Therefore, the incomprehensibility and indefinability of the person of the Holy Spirit are just as valid when they are applied to the Holy Spirit as they are for the other two divine persons (*DH*, 150, 1330).

In Jürgen Bründl, there is no use for the categorical determinant "Here" to specify God's presence among men through the Holy Spirit because of the incomprehensibility of the Holy Spirit. This eschewal stems from the simultaneous necessity of the guidance of the Holy Spirit in order to make the hermeneutic possibility of faith possible and also from God's nonseclusion from man—that is, God's constant interactions with man. The use of the word *Here*, when it comes to God, never implies any discernible clarity and objectivity.[13] Bründl pleads emphatically for the topological metaphor of God's proximity to be taken seriously because it allows for change and an ambiguous, diffuse *différance* regarding certain, actual effects in locating the Holy Spirit.[14] He writes the following about the Holy Spirit: "He remains nearby, even though one can't determine his presence in a specific place. This kind of diffuse proximity leads, epistemologically, to a significant amount of irritation regarding the certainties of faith."[15]

God's divinity is decisively taken into account here because God isn't required to subject himself to man's interpretive authority. That would entail objective clarity without demanding the opening of a new perspective through faith. Man would immediately recognize God through his works and acts of salvation; God would also be unambiguously identifiable and verifiable—that is, differentiated from others.[16] This would mean that man's power to interpret *where*, *when*, and *how* God acts in the world would be relativized and that man's investigations into these questions would always remain contentious and ambiguous. However, God's will for salvation—*why* God acts in the world and turns toward man—is not

13. See Bründl, 14–15.
14. See Bründl, 39.
15. Bründl, 39.
16. Bründl doesn't draw any overhasty, submissive conclusions from man's diffuse, epistemological position toward God. To the contrary, Bründl views this as an opportunity to further the discussion of God's potential power, from a theological perspective, so that direct appeals neither to God's will nor to man's carrying out God's will, in a violent or self-glorifying way, exist. See Bründl, 19, 64.

affected by this relativizing.[17] By using the aforementioned topological metaphor, one can imagine an unfathomable simultaneity and ambiguity of proximity and distance, as well as presence and absence; in this context, one can even apply comparisons of proximity while recognizing that man will never reach God. Due to his love of man, God is more intimate with man through the Holy Spirit than man could ever imagine.[18]

Faith is therefore formulated as a paradoxical situation that man experiences as an imposition from outside. Initially, faith is only granted to man by grace as a gift from God. It is therefore inaccessible to man, and he can't control it; faith can only be accepted or rejected. Reflection about faith itself is secondary; it is only possible after the existential leap of faith through accepting the gift of grace. One can see the precariousness of the state of faith and its far-reaching implications in current reflections, especially in the assertion that unambiguous, totally objective statements can't be made about God (i.e., in a manner that can never be falsified). To the contrary, such statements must always be viewed as relative statements due to God's incomprehensibility and greatness.

However, this doesn't in any way speak in favor of pneumatological solipsism having the final word because God's intrusion into man's reality never happens in a way that man can immediately understand; this would suggest a quality of obsession, on the one hand, and allow one to disregard man's freedom, on the other. Using Jacques Lacan's terminology, in this context, one could say that the breaking forth of the Real must be transferred over to the Symbolic order so that man can manage it. This intellectual attempt at reflection as a way of transitioning to the Symbolic order always relies on social-historical connectedness. The words are not only socially conditioned by their contingent temporality, but God's intervention only appears in traces that, in part, themselves refer back to cryptic traces and point to the need for future interpretations through human discourse.

The Emmaus episode (Luke 24:13–35) illustrates this very well. Two apostles who "stood still, looking sad" (Luke 24:17), leave Jerusalem and move to Emmaus. Jesus joins them; he doesn't force himself on them by announcing who he is but instead interprets Scripture to them and explains, using third-person pronouns, the fate that necessarily awaits him. However, the apostles continue in their state

17. See Bründl, 38.
18. See Bründl, 15.

of sluggishness (Traurigsein) due to their sadness. The information that the women share—that the tomb is empty—is of course heard, but it isn't believed; man's limited perspective isn't transgressed because the apostles hold on to their doubt.[19] François Bovon comments on this passage as follows: "For faith, everything is clear: the Scripture and Jesus' fate. For doubt, everything is obscure: the sense of Scripture and the sense of Jesus' destiny."[20] Jesus continues to walk with them, but he doesn't force himself upon them by introducing himself. The moment of recognition doesn't begin with a categorical shift but is prepared for when "they urged him strongly" (Luke 24:29) to stay with them. According to Bovon, their reference to the fact that it is almost the end of the day isn't the primary reason for their request;[21] one can conclude from their plea that they have a new attitude of openness and a desire to understand. The recognition process finally begins when they break bread together, though only a trace of Jesus is evident here; immediately thereafter, he once again conceals himself in absence—that is, is absent. This indicates a highly ambivalent, dialectical relationship between presence and absence wherein the apostles are unable and remain unable to immediately comprehend and understand Jesus.[22] He exists for the apostles only as a trace and only appears to them as a vestigial presence that anticipates a secondary stage of reciprocal, intersubjective interpretation. This explains why the apostles ask each other, "Were not our hearts burning within us while he was talking to us on the road, while he was opening the scriptures to us?" (Luke 24:32).

It is not immediately clear from Jesus's humanity (Menschsein) that he is the Son of God because this would mean that man would confront the Absolute in an immediate way. According to Gerhard Ludwig Müller, the following is much more important for God's self-revelation in Jesus Christ: "The eternal Word, i.e., God, entered the Here and Now of this world in the person of Jesus of Nazareth and under the conditions of human experience."[23] Even when Müller subsequently refers to "God's immediacy towards man,"[24] this is—as paradoxical as it may sound—not

19. See François Bovon, *Luke 3: A Commentary on the Gospel of Luke, 19:28–24:53*, ed. Helmut Koester, trans. James Crouch (Minneapolis: Fortress, 2012), 374.
20. Bovon, 374.
21. See Bovon, 374.
22. See Bovon, 375.
23. Gerhard Ludwig Müller, *Katholische Dogmatik: Für Studium und Praxis der Theologie* (Freiburg, Germany: Herder, 1995), 48.
24. Müller, *Dogmatik*, 49.

an immediate immediacy but rather God's immediacy toward man that takes place in a human form of immediacy. It is a God-willed unity of immediacy and mediated clarity, willed by God that "through Jesus Christ is . . . the event of immediacy and mediation, both through God's gesture to the world as well as in the world's response, its gesture to God."[25] Jesus Christ is therefore not only a form of mediation but also a mediator all in one person. Furthermore, he is the mediation content itself (DV 2, 972); he prevents situations from arising in which man is constrained in such a way that he would have no choice but to recognize Jesus as Christ. Rather, according to Gerhard Ebeling, the following can be stated about self-revelation: "Revelation, in a theological sense, is an event which pertains to God and man's being together (*Zusammensein*), and, as it were, man's being together (*Zusammensein*) with the world."[26] Following this line of argumentation, Otmar Meuffels writes that the experience and revelation of God in the world and for the world take place within creation; the world, with all its contingencies, and man, in his finiteness, are precisely the localities where God intrudes through his self-revelation without losing his divinity.[27] God is therefore located in *différance* to the world without ending up in an isolated position of pure transcendence. To the contrary, the relationship between God and the world is characterized by a transcendental immanence. In regard to the relationship of différance between God and the world, one can say that God is the abiding, unifying reason and the foundational force in the world who does not level the differences of the world but retains them. God can also be the enduring, unifying reason of différance through his Trinitarian being. From these reflections, it is not surprising that Meuffels incorporates Derrida into his theological ideas in order to show that the différance in the world can be a possible reason for experiencing God.[28] Nevertheless, from a Christian perspective, we must go further than Derrida because while tracking God's traces—that is, deconstructing God's metaphysics—man ends up in a movement of infinite regress that asserts that there is never only a trace of the Absolute; instead, a trace leads to another trace that leads to another trace that

25. Müller, 49.
26. Gerhard Ebeling, *Dogmatik des christlichen Glaubens*, vol. 1, *Prolegomena. Erster Teil. Der Glaube an Gott, den Schöpfer der Welt* (Tübingen, Germany: Mohr Siebeck, 1979), 249.
27. See Otmar Meuffels, Gott *Erfahren: Theologisch-philosophische Bausteine zur Gotteslehre* (Tübingen, Germany: Mohr Siebeck, 2006), 12. See also Bründl, *Nähe*, 78.
28. See Meuffels, Gott, 41.

leads to another trace that leads to another trace.[29] Derrida introduces the neologism différance in an effort to avoid and reveal egregious reductionism by *overly simple* explanations that can result from presumptuous interpretive authority and subjective sovereignty over the text—that is, from the interrelated textual web of the human reality of the world.[30] Différance culminates in an intellectually honest examination of worldly conditions in which final—supposed—certainties of man's horizon of speech and thought are put into question:

> What we know, or what we would know if it were simply a question here of something to know, is that there has never been, never will be, a unique word, a master-name. This is why the thought of the letter *a* in différance is not the primary prescription or the prophetic annunciation of an imminent and as yet unheard-of nomination. . . . And that one puts into question the name of the name.
>
> There will be no unique name, even if it were the name of Being. And we must think this without *nostalgia*, that is, outside of the myth of a purely maternal or paternal language, a lost native country of thought. On the contrary, we must *affirm* this, in the sense in which Nietzsche puts affirmation into play, in a certain laughter and a certain step of the dance.[31]

Yet despite God's withdrawal and direct absence from the world, the following is axiomatic of self-revelation for Christian faith: "By divine revelation God has chosen to manifest and communicate both himself and the eternal decrees of his will for the salvation of humankind, 'so as to share those divine treasures which totally surpass human understanding'" (DV 6, 973).[32]

The initial reaching out comes from God and can't be deduced by man. God's intrusion into man's reality must be regarded as "an experience of an entirely

29. See Derrida, "Différance," 23–26. See also Jacques Derrida, *Writing and Difference*, trans. Alan Bass (Chicago: University of Chicago Press, 1978), 11–13, 71–72, 174–73, 278–92; and Wendel, "'Nichtsprechendes Sprechen' über Transzendenz," 277–80.
30. See Peter Engelmann, "Einführung: Postmoderne und Dekonstruktion; Zwei Stichwörter zur zeitgenössischen Philosophie," in *Postmoderne und Dekonstruktion: Texte französischer Philosophen der Gegenwart*, ed. Peter Engelmann (Stuttgart, Germany: Reclam, 2007), 26–31.
31. Derrida, "Différance," 27.
32. The quoted passage references the "Dogmatic Constitution of the Catholic Faith" of the First Vatican Council (Tanner, 2:806). See also DH, 3005.

different God"[33] and mustn't be prematurely trivialized to fit into an already existing system that would gloss over God's divine Otherness. God's greatness only appears vestigially and in a fragmentary way within the man-made reality of the world because the qualitative différance alone between the creator and the created prevents the world from having enough space to absorb God's greatness. Besides, the ability to experience God is tied to man's horizon of experience and its possibilities. Thus one must note that it isn't the limits of man's horizon and his own man-made reality that prevents man's experience of God. To the contrary, it is precisely the différance between God and man that makes it possible for man to experience God as active and influential in the world without fearing that God would directly impose himself upon man or that God's divinity would be diminished. The différance in the man-made reality of the world is the space where God can reveal himself to his created counterpart: "But nevertheless, it must be made perfectly clear that these secondary conditions are the modes of communication and experience of this God, who only reveals himself in the *différance* between God himself and the experientially conditioned determinacy of this God."[34]

Within the space of man's horizon of experience, God presents himself to man in such a way that he can be experienced in all his greatness and mystery—as a trace and in a trace. Trinitarian theology can be particularly helpful in describing how the Christian God presents and reveals himself to man, especially in terms of différance, without trivializing or glossing over the differences. God's being can be interpreted as the space where a personal différance event of love takes place without ranking divine persons based on their individual personhoods and dignity. This is a diverse space of unity; it has sufficient greatness to also let the différance of the greatest greatness—God's différance—remain in existence as différance and embed the common origin of the Father and Son in the emerging acknowledgment of their love.[35] The différance event of love between the Father and the Son becomes a unifying and enduring bond through the person of the Holy Spirit, who is even able to unify the différance between the world and God without glossing over the differences. The Holy Spirit's gift to the world, through

33. Meuffels, *Gott*, 11.
34. Meuffels, 46.
35. See Bründl, *Nähe*, 111–12. See also Meuffels, *Gott*, 178, 45.

grace, makes it possible for man to have faith; from the perspective of faith, with the support of the Holy Spirit, man can thereby experience God's proximity in his traces.[36]

There is likewise a reference here to a pneumatological solipsism that even provides pneumatological support for not interpreting God's traces as transcendental, superhuman knowledge; rather, the Holy Spirit presents the possibility of interpreting the *traces* as *God's trace*. The différance in the trace persists and therefore remains *ambiguous*, but the Holy Spirit, as a community-unifying force, makes it possible for God's traces to become *interpretable* to man through the communal *togetherness* (Zusammensein) of the faithful, as the Emmaus episode makes clear.[37] The ambiguities of God's traces challenge man's ability to read and then interpret them; God's traces are present as proof of his absent proximity, but they are neither self-explanatory nor interpretable. Man must therefore be granted (i.e., must have) the means to acquire his own set of concepts so that he can introduce his interpretation to the interpretive community—the church's space for discourse.[38]

An interpretation that is made from a purely subjective point of view is no longer an interpretation; to the contrary, it is an unambiguous correction to the meaning of a text. Therefore, whoever removes himself from a specific interpretive community and tells the world that there is one definitive meaning of a text places himself, through this one defiant gesture, in a position of sovereignty *above* the text and *in opposition to* uncomprehending Others. He places himself in the position of an interpretive authority. When Roland Barthes proclaimed the death of the author, he was concerned that the writer of a work isn't an "author" because he doesn't

36. See Meuffels, Gott, 221, 55–56.
37. See Meuffels: God's Trinitarian being surpasses an ever-definitive understanding. Instead, God reveals himself in traces, but these traces stay open for interpretation "in order to identify the trace of *veritas semper maior*, that grew out of *différance*, with the God of Christian faith, who mustn't be understood simply as a categorically identifiable object of our experience, because he would otherwise immediately fall prey to Kant's critique of epistemology. This God, in whom an experienced person is allowed to participate, would then be the transcendental reason for man's ability to enter into a dialogically-responsorial relationship with reality, and in the process be obligated to claims of truth" (53).
38. See Meuffels, 177–78, 186–87. See also Ulrich H. J. Körtner, *Einführung in die theologische Hermeneutik* (Darmstadt, Germany: Wissenschaftliche Buchgesellschaft, 2006), 81.

have authority over the interpretation of the words he uses;[39] he considered this analogous to the authority of the reader—although Barthes wanted to place the reader fully in the center of reception as a placeholder, not based on their personal perspective.[40] One does not have authority over a contingent system of signs if one is inextricably tied to the system in a contingent way.

Analysis and interpretation are always a temporally conditioned communal process; analysis is based on a radical subjectivity that fails to recognize one's own historicity and one's own ties to an interpretive community that can be envisioned as large enough to encompass all speakers of a language. Ongoing analysis and explanation of the world come about through speech because language is man's instrument par excellence for embedding the conditions of the reality of the world in a *logical* horizon.

As mentioned earlier, one mustn't ignore the communal dimension in the analysis of God's traces in order to avoid taking a position of interpretive authority toward a biblical text in an (implicit or explicit) defiant gesture. I will elaborate on the pneumatological foundation of the communal dimension for understanding faith. According to Johannine theology, it is the Holy Spirit of Truth—that is, the παράκλητος—who "will guide you into all the truth" (John 16:13).[41] But the Holy Spirit isn't granted to an individual as a supporter and comforter but is always a gift from God to the community; God can thereby lead the apostles themselves—that is, the Johannine community that listens to the gospel—to the truth.[42] It is also confirmed in DV 4 (973) that the Holy Spirit himself doesn't share any additional revelation about Jesus Christ, who is of course God himself and who has demonstrated to man, in a mediated form, God's magnificence through his abundance of grace, according

39. See Roland Barthes, "The Death of the Author," in *Image, Music, Text*, trans. Stephen Heath (New York: Hill and Wang, 1977), 146–48:

> In the multiplicity of writing, everything is to be *disentangled*, nothing *deciphered*; the structure can be followed, "run" (like the thread of a stocking) at every point and at every level, but there is nothing beneath: the space of writing is to be ranged over, not pierced; writing ceaselessly posits meaning ceaselessly to evaporate it, carrying out a systematic exemption of meaning. In precisely this way literature (it would be better from now on to say *writing*), by refusing to assign a "secret," an ultimate meaning, to the text (and to the world as text), liberates what may be called an anti-theological activity, an activity that is truly revolutionary. (147)

40. See Barthes, 148.
41. See also John 14:16–17; 14:26; 15:26–27; 16:7–11; 16:13–15.
42. See Rudolf Schnackenburg, *The Gospel according to St. John*, vol. 3, *Commentary on Chapters 13–21*, trans. David Smith and G. A. Kon (New York: Crossroad, 1982), 133.

to the prologue to the Gospel of John: "No new public revelation is to be expected before the glorious manifestation of our lord Jesus Christ." The Holy Spirit guides man into the whole truth—that is, he always accompanies man's learning process in regard to the mystery of God. The Holy Spirit doesn't seal this knowledge in a way that would bring a fixed ending to the movement toward perfection. The Holy Spirit assists man in actualizing the mystery of salvation that has been offered to him in his current conditions and circumstances; the spirit assists him in establishing a new, appropriate relationship—that is, a new adequacy:

> The "truth" to which the Paraclete leads the disciples or into which he accompanies them can only be understood in the same sense as in the rest of the gospel—as the revelation brought by Jesus Christ and promising life. . . . It is concerned with a more profound penetration into the content of revelation and at the same time with the application of that revelation to the behavior of the community within the world. . . .
>
> The Paraclete will not, in other words, proclaim anything with a new content. All that he will do is to expound anew to the community Jesus' message in the situation in which that community finds itself and set forth what is coming to it. His guiding the community into all the truth, then, can be seen as an instruction by means of which Christ's revelation can be understood more and more perfectly in each historical context and the community's life can be more and more nourished by it.[43]

The process of reaching a deeper, more satisfactory understanding of truth affects not only an individual's relationship to God but also the entire community of believers. The message from the Holy Spirit is therefore always located in a collective horizon—that is, addressed to a larger audience: "he will guide you into all the truth" (John 16:13), "he will give you another Advocate" (John 14:16), or "when the Advocate comes, whom I will send to you" (John 15:26).

Medard Kehl sees a common origin of unity and différance in the inner Trinitarian event as well as in the ecclesiastical community of believers.[44] In Augustine's relational Trinitarian theology, the Holy Spirit is a unifying bond of love and also

43. Schnackenburg, 3:134–35.
44. See Medard Kehl, *Die Kirche: Eine katholische Ekklesiologie* (Dettelbach, Germany: Röll, 2009), 74–75.

the location where the love of the divine *communio* is actualized. For Kehl, there is a close connection between the divine *communio* and the ecclesiastical *communio*: both are acts of the Holy Spirit. Differences, here, aren't due to a temporary lack of knowledge; they have always been embedded in God's larger intention toward unity. This plurality can grant a unity, even in the church, that is supported by a common origin because by independently imposing its own conditions, this element of plurality becomes constitutive of its own essence. Perspectival differences aren't glossed over; to the contrary, with the assistance of the Holy Spirit, they can be taken seriously through God's greatness and being and can be integrated into a highly dynamic, deep understanding. Even though God—that is, the understandable concept of God—always exceeds man's ability to speak and understand ("id ipsum, quo maius cogitari non potest"),[45] this doesn't require man to remain perpetually on the same level in his knowledge of God. With the assistance of the Holy Spirit, man's capacity for understanding has been given a relative amount of space in which he can delve further into the connections between God and the world.

The multiple interpretive layers of the Bible, especially of the Old Testament, that modern exegesis has uncovered are clear evidence that man's knowledge of God started with God's initial intrusion into human reality (according to Kant, the intervention of the Absolute; according to Lacan, the intrusion of the Real). However, the task of understanding the event of God and translating it through language into a symbolic structure that is relevant to man's everyday world subsequently becomes the responsibility of the interpretive community of believers. Pure wonder remains static, it fades, and it is ultimately forgotten. Doctrinal history and ongoing theological research are eloquent testimony to the fact that man's efforts—his desire to understand—haven't yet come to an end and that the interpretive community of the church continues to thrive.

45. Anselm of Canterbury, *Proslogion*, trans. M. J. Charlesworth (Notre Dame, IN: University of Notre Dame Press, 1979), 16.

The Testimony of Faith

The Subjective Relationship to Truth: Paul in His Contemporary Horizon

Let's take a step back and ask about the conditions of the act of faith itself—but not from a theological horizon. This has already been touched on from an Augustinian perspective; in that context, the problem of grace and its granting became, to a certain extent, readily apparent. It must also be emphasized that one must never ignore Paul's statement about God in Romans 11, if one assumes that the Holy Spirit is the defining element of a Christian's ability to believe and that the Holy Spirit is owed the same divine dignity and greatness as is given to God himself:

> O the depth of the riches and wisdom and knowledge of God! How unsearchable are his judgments and how inscrutable his ways!
>
> For who has known the mind of the Lord?
> Or who has been his counselor?
> Or who has given a gift to him,
> to receive a gift in return?
>
> For from him and through him and to him are all things. (Rom 11:33–36)[46]

As believers *and* rational human beings, it is not our place to look directly at God's decisions about grace. It might be worthwhile to consider a different perspective toward the act of grace, one that doesn't ask about the *how* but rather attempts to describe *the fact that*. Alain Badiou investigates the question, At what point can one call a person a subject? He begins his exploration with an event that just appears and lacks compelling proof (i.e., according to Lacan, a Real event) even though the individual declares and pledges fidelity to it.

46. See also Isaiah's statement: "Who has directed the spirit of the Lord, or as his counselor has instructed him? Whom did he consult for his enlightenment, and who taught him the path of justice? Who taught him knowledge, and showed him the way of understanding?" (Isa 40:13–14).

In order to be able to place Badiou's observations about Paul into his larger intellectual horizon, it is necessary to first examine his observations about ontology and the structure of Being (Seinsstruktur). It is no surprise that Badiou indicates that he followed Heidegger's teachings in his early works.[47] He states that he then turned away from Heidegger's path and left Heidegger's examination of Being (Sein) in poetics and attempted, instead, to trace this discourse on ontology back to mathematics and its representation of Being (Sein). Whereas poetic discourse about ontology, according to Heidegger, accepts the truth within the situation of Being (Sein) as a surplus of presence that reveals itself and appears to the observer,[48] Badiou begins by expanding the situation so that an event that is located on the edge of the situation, and points to the truth, can take place (because it is subject to chance), but the truth itself does not belong to the given situation. Therefore, the truth is located outside the inventoried situation but nevertheless obeys the same rules as all the other elements found in the situation.[49] For this reason, it is impossible for the person who finds himself in this situation to say whether this truth does or doesn't exist; he can only believe in it because the truth isn't presented as an element in the situation (it isn't an element of the situation) but rather exists only—if at all—as a representation (as a real name, as it were, as a signifier without a signified), and the truth is therefore indistinguishable from the situation:[50] "In reality, an inhabitant of S can only *believe* in the existence of an indiscernible—insofar as if it exists, it is outside the world."[51]

This is the point where Heidegger and Badiou meet and then part ways. According to Badiou, truth, in a temporal sense, is a future moment that will appear or reveal itself—that is, will have appeared.[52] Truth is not an object at man's disposal, conceptually or objectively. For Heidegger, man is in a situation of receptive, observing openness in which the truth comes to light as a revelation and a disclosure within

47. See Badiou, *Being and Event*, 10.
48. See Badiou, 9–10. See also Martin Heidegger, "The Origin of the Work of Art," in *Basic Writings*, ed. David Farrell Krell (New York: HarperCollins, 2008), 195–203.
49. Badiou designates this as a "generic" concept that is located outside the situation—due to its expansion—but is tied to all elements of the situation and is subject to the same rules. Truth can, however, rearrange and restructure the elements of the situation (statement of the domination of the truth); this explains why he also calls the truth "generic." See also Badiou, *Being and Event*, 327, 372.
50. See Badiou, *Being and Event*, 396.
51. Badiou, 373.
52. See Martin Heidegger, "On the Essence of Truth," in Krell, *Basic Writings*, 124–35; see also Badiou, *Being and Event*, 397–98, 400.

the space of Being (Sein); the truth of a Being (Seienden) appears when this Being reveals itself to be moving away from concealment and a situation that has been veiled to a position of openness: "To engage oneself with the disclosedness of beings is not to lose oneself in them; rather, such engagement withdraws in the face of beings in order that they might reveal themselves with respect to what and how they are, and in order that presentative correspondence might take its standard from them. As this letting-be it exposes itself to beings as such and transposes all comportment into the open region. Letting-be, i.e., freedom is intrinsically exposing, ek-sistent. Considered in regard to the essence of truth, the essence of freedom manifests itself as exposure to the disclosedness of beings."[53]

Thus, for Heidegger, truth can be understood as the moment of revelation itself, in which essence shows itself, in its unconcealment, to someone who encounters it with openness. The difference between Heidegger and Badiou can be found here.[54] For Heidegger, truth is an intimate element of Being (Sein) where the essence of a Being (Seiendes) appears in its unconcealment. For Badiou, truth is in its appearance (as a real locality) outside the situation—that is, in the expanded situation; it is not an element of the world but is rather a future moment. In anticipation of this moment, one puts oneself in an ongoing relationship of fidelity to it, if one believes in the existence of truth. The individual who has professed his faith, therefore, speaks about the truth in the future perfect verb tense—that it will have appeared. This person has accepted a radical perspective of subjectivity that is fundamentally different from an external perspective because this person considers the situation closed—that is, not expanded. Truth will not have become visible because it doesn't exist for such a person.[55]

From a Christian point of view, one must urgently introduce a corrective element into Badiou's way of speaking about future revelation in the future perfect tense. The truth has already been disclosed and entered into reality through Jesus Christ's self-revelation. Christ's message is radically different from the message of John the Baptist; John the Baptist postpones the dawning of the kingdom of God

53. Heidegger, "Essence of Truth," 125–26.

54. In Heidegger, truth is to be understood less as an all-encompassing horizon to which one is answerable and must confess. To be sure, Heidegger recognizes Being (das Sein) as an all-encompassing horizon that remains closed to man through ontological *différance* because man as a Being (Seiender) only has another Being (Seiendes) as a point of access to his understanding of Being (Seinsverständnis); man is never Being (das Sein) itself. See Heidegger, *Being and Time*, 10–13, 41–44.

55. See Badiou, *Being and Event*, 396–400.

to the future at hand so that he, to some extent, through his call to repent, connects the certainty of judgment by fire with the certainty of inescapability—the trial by fire will have raged (Matt 3:1–12). Jesus's message of the kingdom of God basically reverses the time structure because John the Baptist's use of the imperative mood and verb tense structure—indicative mood / future perfect tense—isn't valid for him (summons to repentance—arrival of the day of judgment): "The time is fulfilled, and the kingdom of God has come near; repent, and believe in the good news" (Mark 1:15).

The time structure here is closer to the following sequence: indicative (dawning of the kingdom of God), *followed* by the imperative mood for the call to repent. The end of time has already begun; therefore, the Old Testament pattern of promise and future fulfillment does not apply because the person and message of Jesus Christ directly prepare the way for the unfolding of God's kingdom in the present time period (Luke 11:10; 17:20). Alain Badiou and Giorgio Agamben differ in their exegesis of Paul on this point. Time continues to have a chronological structure for Badiou, and even one's own fidelity to the event doesn't bring with it any time-altering repentance; it remains, to a certain extent, a time of waiting and hope for a new beginning in the future. In contrast, according to Agamben, *messianic time* is specifically characterized by the end of chronological time.[56] Thus Paul isn't a prophet; to the contrary, he must be understood as an apostle and no longer as a prophet:

> Each time the prophets announce the coming of the Messiah, the message is always about a time to come, a time not yet present. This is what marks the difference between the prophet and the apostle. The apostle speaks forth from the arrival of the Messiah. At this point prophecy must keep silent, for now prophecy is truly fulfilled. . . . The word passes on to the apostle, to the emissary of the Messiah, whose time is no longer the future, but the present. This is why Paul's technical term for the messianic

56. See Dominik Finkelde, *Politische Eschatologie nach Paulus: Badiou–Agamben–Žižek–Santner* (Vienna: Turia + Kant, 2007), 49–55. The differences between Badiou and Agamben can't be treated in a comprehensive way within the parameters of this work. However, Finkelde presents them in great detail; the different concepts of the "subject" that these two philosophers have in reference to Paul are especially fascinating. Badiou makes the subject in the event into a central issue in human reality, whereas Agamben splits the subject and defines it in relationship to the Messiah (46–48, et passim).

> event is *ho nyn kairos*, “the time of the now”; this is why Paul is an apostle and not a prophet.[57]

In order to better understand Badiou’s theories, his ontological analysis has to be further explicated. He begins with foundational axioms and deduces his ontological conclusions from them in a logical, deductive way; in doing so, he repeatedly suggests that one needn’t follow the details of his axiomatic framework. But if one does follow his system, it takes on the character of a decision; this will be of importance for the concept of an event that is based on a relationship of fidelity.[58]

It is foundational for the analysis of Being (Seinsanalyse) in a mathematical domain, according to Badiou, that Being presents itself as a defined space that is in principle a void set and is only secondarily filled with multiple elements. It is axiomatic for his mathematical approach to ontology that a filled space does not exist but rather that, in principle, the void “exists” before filling up and that this void set should be viewed neither as the void Being (Sein) nor as the plurality of unfilled multiplicities (as a plural form of void sets) because nothingness knows no law of difference.[59] However, this can only be recognized through the operation of counting or subtraction.[60] Pure, orderless multiplicity will be counted, and thereby structured, as *one* element by someone who is counting; prior to this counting, the elements are unstructured and orderless. Only conscious counting establishes the situation as multiplicity because there was no awareness of difference and, therefore, no recognition of multiplicity prior to this counting process.[61] However, because multiplicity continues to prevail, it is the responsibility of a counting agent to define an inner and an outer and to determine what the situation is—that is, what

57. Giorgio Agamben, *The Time That Remains: A Commentary on the Letter to the Romans*, trans. Patricia Dailey (Stanford, CA: Stanford University Press, 2005), 61.
58. For example, Badiou declares the following about the multiple structure of Being (Sein) in *Being and Event*: “The thesis of the infinity of being is necessarily an ontological decision, which is to say an axiom. Without such a decision it will remain for ever possible for being to be essentially finite” (148). Badiou does not want to advocate for arbitrariness in one’s choice of words; to the contrary, he wants to show that in fidelity to one’s own decisions, one must also take responsibility for the consequences.
59. See Badiou, *Being and Event*, 66–69. See also Badiou: “The truth is rather this: the unicity of the void-set is immediate because nothing differentiates it, not because its difference can be attested. An irremediable unicity based on in-difference is herein substituted for unicity based on difference. . . . There are not ‘several’ voids, there is only one void” (68–69).
60. See Badiou, 67.
61. So this one situation can never exist because the structuring of a situation only happens subsequently by counting the multiple elements, even though the elements are never totally countable. This explains why its constitution indicates a clear outer and inner of what belongs to the situation.

belongs to the situation as it is defined and what doesn't. The defined situation therefore appears as closed because of exclusions.[62]

Badiou begins his analysis of the defined situation from an inner perspective that is characterized by a constructivist point of view. From an inner perspective, the situation and knowledge about it—that is, the naming possibilities—are complete and encyclopedic; the inner perspective is complete and closed and therefore possesses a complete set of rules that differentiates between what is legal and illegal:[63] "Knowledge calms the passion of being: measure taken of excess, it tames the state, and unfolds the infinity of the situation within the horizon of a constructive procedure shored up on the already-known."[64] This becomes problematic for the definition of a situation at a decisive point, the emergence of an event. The event, by necessity, finds a site within the state of a situation, without the event itself belonging to the situation; to the contrary, it is an intrusion from outside. Hence the evental site can be viewed as a precipitating moment because it is on the edge of the situation and on the edge of the void—that is, of the excluded/unnamable:[65] "A site is therefore the *minimal* effect of structure which can be conceived; it is such that it belongs to the situation, whilst what belongs to it in turn does not."[66]

Badiou uses the example of the French Revolution to clarify this further. The evental site of the revolution is France in the final years of the eighteenth century; the French Revolution as an event itself is neither part of nor an element in this situation. The Revolution is a random element, intruding from the outside, that can't be deduced from the current conditions and rules of pre-Revolutionary France.[67] From an ontological perspective, and using the conceptual work of the axiom of the void, the event can be described as follows: "The event is thus clearly the multiple which both presents its entire site, and, by means of the pure signifier of itself immanent to its own multiple, manages to present the presentation itself, that is, the one of the infinite multiple that it is."[68]

62. See Badiou, *Being and Event*, 95, 98–99; see also Badiou: "The state of a situation is the riposte to the void obtained by the count-as-one of its parts. This riposte is apparently complete, since it both numbers what the first structure allows to in-exist . . . and, finally, it generates the One-One by numbering structural completeness itself" (98).
63. See Badiou, 286–94.
64. Badiou, 294. Hence the state of a situation appears as a closed, coherent system.
65. See Badiou, 175, 19.
66. Badiou, 175.
67. See Badiou, 180–82.
68. Badiou, 180.

The event is thus that factor that makes a complete inventory of the previous situation and reconnects it with elements that had earlier been outside—in other words, excluded (i.e., they weren't recognized or named until now). The previous situation was summarized as a defined situation. But if one now accepts the intrusion of the event from outside, then the state of the inventoried situation is the only one that endures; yet the event presents itself as a superordinate inventory and an escalating order. The event is therefore the ultraone.[69]

But now we come to the crux of Badiou's entire ontology that is suddenly of great importance: How does one come to the knowledge that an event has taken place? Or to ask this question more pointedly, following Badiou's line of thinking, How does one become a subject?

Before we can answer this question, we must return to the problem of the closedness of the state of the situation. One can't determine if the intrusion of the event took place from the inventory of the situation because the inventoried situation doesn't have a way to name or recognize the event: For the sake of preserving the status quo of the situation, the event never took place. The inventory thereby imprints a strictly deductive system of logic onto the inventoried situation that can't be transgressed from within. The constructiveness of the inventory creates the rules and naming possibilities from within because the moment is also situated here that takes over counting as one—that is, the operation of counting to restructure. The event has neither presentation nor naming because it comes from outside and is a chance occurrence:[70] "Furthermore, within the constructivist vision of being, and this is a crucial point, there is no place for an event to take place. . . . Constructivism has no need to decide upon the non-being of the event, because it does not have to know anything of the latter's undecidability. . . . In the case of the evental ultra-one, the operation does not operate, and this is quite enough for contructivist thought to deny any being to what thereby leads the authority of language into an impasse. . . . Unconstructible, the event is not. Inasmuch as it exceeds the immanence of language to the situation, intervention is unthinkable."[71]

69. See Badiou, 182.
70. See Žižek, *Ticklish Subject*, 137–39.
71. Badiou, *Being and Event*, 289–90. Badiou views Wittgenstein's famous dictum in the *Tractatus Logico-Philosophicus*—"Whereof one cannot speak, thereof one must be silent"—from the perspective of the constraints of language because man's thinking is dependent on language. See Badiou, *Being and Event*, 291.

The event can't be recognized from the inventoried situation; therefore, in order to be able to recognize the event, the inventory has to be transgressed. It reaches a point of radical subjectivity because the individual now becomes a subject.[72] It reaches this point through the subject's decision to take a committed position toward the intrusive event; the subject thereby confirms the existence of the event because the inventoried structure has been transgressed. The event emerges by chance and out of nothingness,[73] and because it can't be recognized and named within the current means, it needs to be named before it can emerge out of anonymity.[74] Thus the "French Revolution" arises out of the illegitimate uprising of the Third Estate against the absolute state and the French king. In the process, it becomes immediately clear that naming is already part of the event itself because the revolt of the Third Estate was still illegal and didn't yet have a name, whereas the "French Revolution" indicates, by its name, that the legitimate relations have already changed *through the internal perspective of the Revolution*.[75]

The event takes place—that is, has a starting point—when the individual *decides*, in a subsequent step, that the event does exist and then, in an act of interpretation, gives it a name: this makes it into a subject.[76] Badiou calls this stance of actively wanting to be involved an "intrusion"—that is, an "intervention." The stance of "fidelity" attaches itself to this intervention; this makes it clear that the event wasn't just a passing flare-up of an illusory desire. The event will be permanently valid because it has transformed the previous situation into a new structure.[77] Through this restructuring capability that is connected to its permanent validity, the event brings about a new knowledge position for those involved—that is, for those intervening. A new horizon of knowledge and understanding is opened with the decision in favor of the event: "For an established political Order, the revolutionary turmoil that threatens to overthrow it is a chaotic dislocation, while from the viewpoint

72. See Žižek, *Ticklish Subject*, 141–42.
73. See Badiou, *Being and Event*, 196.
74. See Badiou, 203–7.
75. See Žižek, *Ticklish Subject*, 130.
76. See Badiou, *Being and Event*, 205–6, 221, 230. See also Žižek, *Ticklish Subject*: "The subject comes *after* the Event and persists in discerning its traces within his situation" (130). The reason one has decided in favor of the event is also a secondary factor, since one had to first decide in favor of the event perspective so that one could recognize its existence. One can then give the reasons one decided in favor of it. See also Badiou, *Being and Event*, 220–21.
77. See Badiou, 202–10, 212–19.

of the Revolution, *ancien régime* itself is a name for disorder, for an impenetrable and ultimately 'irrational despotism.'"[78]

This results in a categorial division in perspective and therefore, in a manner of speaking, in a shibboleth in language and knowledge. The internal perspective is only understandable from within and therefore also correct; the external perspective is only understandable from without—as the not-inner—and therefore also legal.[79] Both perspectives are incommensurable because they fundamentally diverge.

Badiou sees the truth event par excellence in the Christ event, especially in the Pauline interpretation and in Paul himself. His entire focus is on the Christ event of the resurrection that, according to Badiou, constitutes the core of Christ's message.[80] According to Badiou, the Pauline gesture of an immediate decision to declare that the truth event of Christ's resurrection from the dead had occurred stands out as an example of becoming a subject. The radical subjectivity that emerges from this decision is neither discussed nor pondered. It also isn't carried over onto Paul from the outside through a mediating factor; it comes from outside and directly affects Paul's inwardness, through grace alone.[81] Through this act of decision, the individual's status changes and he becomes a subject.[82] How one arrives at faith—that is, at the recognition that the event has taken place—can of course be declared through the concept of grace; however, in principle, it remains *logically* indescribable. This explains Badiou's use of Lacan's concept of the Real in this context.[83] The truth event of Christ is an occurrence that intrudes from the outside and invalidates the existing order as soon as one recognizes it as the truth, decides in favor of this truth, and commits to it. The event can't be logically deduced because that would mean that

78. Žižek, *Ticklish Subject*, 138.
79. See Žižek, 136.
80. See Badiou, *Saint Paul*, 4, 33–34, 45. Badiou isn't by any means endorsing Christian theism here; to the contrary, he describes the resurrection itself as a "fable." Nevertheless, he sees in Paul's gesture an ideal example of becoming a subject in its radicality. What he was repeatedly criticized for under the guise of "defrocking grace" appears to Žižek more as an advantage than a disadvantage. See also Žižek, *On Belief*, 112–13, 144–45.
81. See Badiou, *Saint Paul*, 4, 13–15, 48–50.
82. See Žižek, *Ticklish Subject*, 158–59.
83. See Badiou, *Saint Paul*, 55–56, 66, 108.

the earlier logic continued to remain valid. But then the event wouldn't happen and wouldn't be real.[84]

It is impossible to describe and explain the event through the prevailing discourse because it transgresses and restructures the current condition—in fact, the prevailing discourses are declared invalid (1 Cor 1:18–25): the logical wisdom discourse of the Greeks doesn't allow for the possibility of access to the Christ event, just as Jewish discourse lacks the necessary signs for the verification of God's intrusion.[85] The importance of the shibboleth logic of the resurrection becomes evident here: if you believe in the resurrection and therefore accept an internal perspective, then a new, transcendent knowledge arises that appears to make the restructuring of the constitution of Being (Sein) understandable. In contrast, if one considers the event of the cross and resurrection to be foolishness and scandalous, it will be a source of irritation. Because the logical wisdom discourse is expired, the concepts and tools of this discourse are irrelevant to making the truth event understandable; one would fall back into the perspective of the mythological regime toward human knowledge and reason. Therefore, Badiou emphasizes the following in order to clarify the distinction between Greek philosophy and Christian truth: Paul is an antiphilosopher who strictly represents antiphilosophy because the logical wisdom discourse of the message that he has accepted has become invalid.

Philosophy doesn't have the status of an error or an illusion for Paul. What is much more significant to him is the overcoming of philosophy's dominance and validity; for the community of believers, philosophy has been superseded and its validity has been invalidated.[86] The subversion of this newly won knowledge of the event leads here[87] because it can restructure and tie together the available elements. In mathematical diction, Christ is the ultraone and the universal

84. See Finkelde, *Eschatologie*, 31–32, 103, 113, 115. Although Finkelde indicates that the event can be understood as Real, in the Lacanian sense, only for Žižek but not for Badiou, I'd like to suggest that one can also view the event as Real for Badiou. In the first place, Badiou himself introduces the concept of the Real, and second, the event can't be forced from within. This is what differentiates the authentic event (the French Revolution or Christ's resurrection) from the pseudoevent (National Socialism). See Badiou, *Being and Event*, 196–97, 290, 381. See also Žižek, *Ticklish Subject*, 200.

85. See Badiou, *Saint Paul*, 40–46.

86. See Badiou, 17, 47, 49–51, 57–58, 83. Badiou: "Simply, that this event is of such a character as to render the philosophical logos incapable of declaring it. The underlying thesis is that one of the phenomena by which one recognizes an event is that the former is like a point of the real [*point de réel*] *that puts language into deadlock*" (46; brackets in the original).

87. See Badiou, 47–48, 50–51.

singularity; in Pauline diction, Christ is the new Adam who reconciles creation anew (Rom 5).[88]

It is impossible to logically deduce the event from the given discourses or preconceived definitions of truth because this event, which intrudes from the outside into the situation, is Real; it can't be discussed because no neutral perspective toward the event exists. The choice of perspective is always already given and can't be abandoned.[89] The authority of faith—that is, of the resurrection—doesn't need or possess any mediating support because authority itself already exists in the act of accepting the decision; hence the philosophers' laughter after the Areopagus sermon doesn't result in any wavering in Paul's convictions, and he also doesn't go to Jerusalem, where the Christian authorities would grant him authority.[90] According to Badiou, grace is granted to Paul without mediation and is therefore a radical-subjective element that neither needs nor can have further authority: validation of the event is lacking because it is an individual's decision to commit to the event.[91]

Even Badiou, despite his plea for radical subjectivity, asks about evidence for recognition of this event. Slavoj Žižek also takes on this problem and recognizes that there is one clear-cut marker that confirms, for Badiou, the validity of the event:

> A true Event emerges out of the "void" of the situation; it is attached to its *élément surnuméraire*, to the symptomatic element that has no proper place in the situation, although it belongs to it, while the simulacrum of an Event disavows the symptom. For this reason, the Leninist October Revolution remains an Event, since it relates to the "class struggle" as the symptomatic torsion of its situation, while the Nazi movement is a simulacrum, a disavowal of the trauma of class struggle. . . . The difference lies not in the inherent qualities of the Event itself, but in its place—in the way it relates to the situation out of which it emerged. As for the external gaze that bears witness to the Truth of the Event, this gaze is able to discern that Truth only in so far as it is the gaze of the individuals who are already engaged on

88. See Badiou, 13–14, 22, 75–76, 95. See Žižek, *Ticklish Subject*, 146–47, 228, 239.
89. See Badiou, *Saint Paul*, 45, 70–71, 96. Even philosophy is not liberated from this choice of perspective; to the contrary, it is bound by its own presuppositions (e.g., idealism vs. phenomenology). See Žižek, *Ticklish Subject*, 133–34.
90. See Badiou, *Saint Paul*, 108–9, 18.
91. See Finkelde, *Eschatology*, 21, 29.

> its behalf: there is no neutral enlightened public opinion to be impressed by the Event, since Truth is discernible only for the potential members of the new Community of "believers," for their engaged gaze.[92]

There is a recognition—that is, a moment of recognition—that confirms the validity of the event, but this recognition occurs at the same time as the choice of perspective; this makes it easy to say that we are dealing with a situation of performative recognition.[93] Because one accepts a perspective by choosing it, one also immediately recognizes the validity of the event; because the validity of the event has been adopted and recognized, one follows this validity in an infinite faithful procedure because one trusts in the validity and the truth of the event.[94] Badiou speaks about the truth as a not yet presented part of the situation—in other words, as something that transgresses the constitution and the given (i.e., existing horizon) but is nevertheless valid. The subject hopes and trusts and doesn't speak about the truth in the *conditional* subjunctive; the subject's language is characterized by speech in the future perfect tense so that, at least in terms of language, there is no doubt about the validity of the event and its truth.[95]

From the standpoint of a theorist who is carrying out an analysis of the truth, the fragility and the state of uncertainty of the event should be emphasized. On the one hand, the event doesn't possess an ontological guarantee that is so deeply rooted that the validity of the event would be visibly persuasive to everyone. The event is extremely fragile and in a precarious condition because it can only gain legitimacy through self-referentiality; it neither has an alternative foundation nor is able to be aligned with the given situation and its inner-worldly logic.[96] On the other hand, the subject trusts the validity of the evental truth, whereby the state

92. Žižek, *Ticklish Subject*, 140. Likewise, Žižek, 158, 182–83. It should be noted here that Žižek is a self-acknowledged neo-Marxist. Just as he actively advocates for a willingness to act on behalf of the repoliticization of politics, he likewise begins here with a view toward the event in order to encourage politics to proactively take the measures that are necessary to restructure the situation. See also Žižek, 221–28, 347–59.
93. See Žižek: "The engaged 'subjective perspective' on the Event is part of the Event itself" (137).
94. See Badiou, *Being and Event*, 336–39.
95. See Badiou, 396–98. See Badiou, *Saint Paul*: "Paul firmly holds to the militant discourse of weakness. The declaration will have no other force than the one it declares and will not presume to convince through the apparel of prophetic reckoning, of the miraculous exception, or of the ineffable personal revelation. It is not the singularity of the subject that validates what the subject says; it is what he says that founds the singularity of the subject" (53).
96. See Badiou, *Saint Paul*, 50.

is restructured and the entire situation gets a new axiomatic framework (instead of the one, the ultraone). A *different* logic emerges from the event (a logic of irretrievable alterity, i.e., the Real); even Badiou admits that a new knowledge emerges here that can, for example, generate the naming of the event or is in a position of a secondary logical deduction.[97]

Consequently, the subject himself is in a precarious state of limbo because he remains embedded in his environment, in the earlier defined situation. An intrusion into the Real only now becomes possible because the subject has transgressed the perspective of the earlier inventoried situation. The subject left it far behind much earlier yet is unable to extricate himself from it: "Finally, a subject is at the intersection, via its language, of knowledge [the content of the site] and truth [the essence of the event]. . . . A subject is a knowledge suspended by a truth whose finite moment it is."[98] The subject doesn't create the truth. Rather, the subject ends up in the process of subjectification so that he proclaims a future moment of truth and thereby transgresses the domain of the universal and the ethical; the subject, not the truth, is the finite element in the situation.[99] Žižek uses Badiou's interpretation of Paul as a contrast to the stance of postmodernity and deconstruction. Instead of the undecidability of ambiguity, where nothing can be definitively determined, Žižek declares with Badiou that there is *only one* truth in a situation with which one either does or doesn't align oneself.[100]

Because the intruding evental truth isn't static but rather has an all-encompassing generic structure, the subject can reallocate more and more elements to the ultraone through its linking and calculating procedure. Through this decision, the subject is bound in fidelity to the event and will act accordingly. Therefore, the Pauline process of fidelity takes place after the event of Christ's resurrection through the act of love. The horizon of the Old Testament and the validity of its law is transgressed through the resurrection, but it is simultaneously reconnected; therefore, love doesn't abolish the validity of the law but instead fulfills it to an even greater degree (Rom 13:8–10).[101] According to Badiou, the occurrence of the event doesn't signify a reworking of what already exists through an expanded or improved logic.

97. See Badiou, *Being and Event*, 252, 396.
98. Badiou, 406.
99. See Badiou, *Saint Paul*, 51–53.
100. See Žižek, *Ticklish Subject*, 131.
101. See Badiou, *Saint Paul*, 89–91.

Rather, the logic of the event is at odds with the established order because its site has been established, but it also simultaneously transgresses it. Because the event by its very nature doesn't correspond to stasis, an individual's declaration of fidelity to the event exists beyond the static and has the quality of a process in which the subject declares his fidelity to the event.[102]

> To be faithful to an event is to move within the situation that this event has supplemented, by *thinking* (although all thought is a practice, a putting to the test) the situation "according" to the event. And this, of course—since the event was excluded by all the regular laws of the situation—compels the subject to *invent* a new way of being and acting in the situation. . . . An evental fidelity is a real break (both thought and practiced) in the specific order within which the event took place (be it political, loving, artistic or scientific . . . [ellipsis in original]). I shall call "truth" (*a* truth) the real process of a fidelity to an event: that which this fidelity *produces* in the situation.[103]

Christ's resurrection isn't an end point in the history of God and man; to the contrary, Christ's resurrection has given man a new beginning because the reign of sin has been broken, and his bond to the law has thereby also been revoked. Through Christ's resurrection, and one's belief in it, man acknowledges that Christ's bond to the law has been revoked and that Christ has been spared the kingdom of sin and death; through Christ's action, man has gained access to eternal life and can live and act freely. For the faithful, there is now only positive freedom because they have faith in the God of love and mercy (1 Cor 6:12).[104] This shows that the decision in favor of the perspective of the resurrection assumes the suitability of the act (through the practice of love). This happens not immediately but rather through a process-like structure in which faith involves a choice of perspective, love involves a decision about reification, and hope involves a state of persistent readiness so that one constantly professes one's faith anew in the resurrection and puts this into

102. See Badiou, 21–23, 47–48, 107–8.
103. Alain Badiou, *Ethics: An Essay on the Understanding of Evil*, trans. Peter Hallward (London: Verso, 2001), 41–42.
104. See Žižek, *Ticklish Subject*, 146–51.

practice through love by living one's life as defined by the resurrection.[105] Because the intrusion—that is, the intervention—and the subsequent declaration of fidelity take up such a large space in Badiou's conception of truth, Žižek places them under the double aspect of the theological-political: "theological in so far as religious revelation is the unavowed paradigm of his notion of the Truth-Event; political because Truth is not a state to be perceived by means of a neutral intuition, but a matter of (ultimately political) engagement. Consequently, for Badiou, subjectivization designates the event of Truth that disrupts the closure of the hegemonic ideological domain and/or the existing social edifice (the Order of Being)."[106]

Badiou has no hesitation advocating for a truth that is objectively inaccessible because it intrudes from outside; this truth can never be easily managed through rational discourse about authority because it will always transgress man's logical horizon.[107] However, it must be noted that his plea for a radical subjectivity without external signs of or a foundation for authority can lead to an excessive degeneration of Christianity or even a fundamentalist orientation. The ineffability of the resurrection—in its antiphilosophical stance that totally defies logical-rational discourse along with its action-oriented declaration of truth without any supporting, external authority—can quickly result in a potential for power that should not be underestimated;[108] this is especially the case when everything is given an activist reading that encourages political action, as in Slavoj Žižek.[109]

Jürgen Bründl focuses on this delicate issue and attempts, due to the objective absence but simultaneous closeness of the Holy Spirit, to totally invalidate

105. See Badiou, *Saint Paul*, 93. See also Žižek, *Ticklish Subject*, 135.

106. Žižek, *Ticklish Subject*, 183. Žižek also links the overcoming of the universal by a radical subjectivity with the revocation of the ethical, as universally understandable, through Kierkegaard's reading of Abraham's sacrifice of Isaac: "The traditional universe is ethical, while the Religious involves a radical disruption of the Old Ways—true religion is a crazy wager on the Impossible we have to make once we lose support in tradition." Žižek, 115. Based on this interpretation, one can likewise understand why Žižek uses Badiou and his reading of Paul as proof of the repoliticizing of the postpolitical (as pure management of the current conditions)—politics as transgression and active event termination of what exists: "The political act (intervention) proper is not simply something that works well within the framework of the existing relations, but something that *changes the very framework that determines how things work*." Žižek, 199.

107. See Badiou, *Saint Paul*, 58–59. The following critique nevertheless seems relevant, although Badiou briefly touches on Marcion's surplus in regard to Pauline theology and also emphasizes the fragility and precariousness of the subjective weakness of faith. See also Badiou, 34–35, 49–53.

108. See Badiou, *Saint Paul*, 46–50, 58–59.

109. See Žižek, *Ticklish Subject*, 199, 221–28. As long as Christian action is only based on love, the Christian subject actually shouldn't be the source of any readiness for violence or straightforward violence. The fact that the history of Christianity nevertheless knows moments of an un-Christian use of violence, within a perspective of legitimacy through faith, nevertheless indicates this danger.

the legitimacy of the power of faith.[110] Because an ultimate justification of faith is lacking and strong metaphysics has become untenable as a consequence of Kant's critique and the deconstruction's critique, Bründl—relying in part on Gianni Vattimo, Jacques Derrida, and Jean-François Lyotard—defends a weak form of truth. Instead of a brutal clarity that, to some extent, doesn't allow for the emergence of an awareness of problems of ambiguity in regard to God and the world, Bründl shows an understanding of theology that doesn't artificially belittle God's greatness for the sake of clarity but makes it available for human concerns.[111] Instead, Bründl emphasizes the possibility that Trinitarianism offers due to the ambivalent relationship between God and the world through the absent immanence of the Holy Spirit. He allows for differences between things to endure while keeping their singularity, and by laying the groundwork for the Trinity, he integrates them into a unifying framework.[112]

In principle, ambiguities should be neither viewed negatively nor considered to be failed interpretations; clarity can also produce a stasis that reaches a firm conclusion based on a defined statement. In contrast, ambiguities release an energy that makes one constantly think experientially about the history of the encounter between God and man and also makes it possible to experience this experiential event oneself.[113] Truth only has a chance of becoming *believable* where man finds it questionable. An ahistorical truth that doesn't affect one's own life horizon is irrelevant because it is remote from life: "To put it succinctly: *Perspectivity is the condition for the possibility of truth.* There is no truth in a 'view from nowhere,' because nothing can be viewed, understood, or judged to be wrong. Where falsehood doesn't factually exist, and can't even exist, there is no need for truth. Truth only becomes important under conditions of finitude and perspectivity. One only needs truth there, and it only exists there. Only where truth is possible, or actually at risk, is there a battle for truth; without this battle, there is no truth."[114]

110. See Bründl, *Nähe*, 18–20, 38–41.
111. See Bründl, 105–8.
112. See Bründl, 15, 19–20, 39–47, 107–12.
113. See Bründl, 39. See also Meuffels, *Gott*, 88.
114. Ingolf U. Dalferth and Philipp Stoellger, "Perspektive und Wahrheit: Einleitende Hinweise auf eine klärungsbedürftige Problemgeschichte," in *Wahrheit in Perspektiven: Probleme einer offenen Konstellation*, ed. Ingolf U. Dalferth and Philipp Stoellger (Tübingen, Germany: Mohr Siebeck, 2004), 13. See also Florian Klug, *Die causa sui im Verhältnis zum unbewegten Beweger: Untersuchungen zum Einfluss der Philosophie des Aristoteles zur Gotteslehre und Schöpfungstheologie Herman Schells* (Münster, Germany: Lit, 2013), 130–35.

Through the a priori condition of human perspectivity—that is, that only one contingent view of reality exists—truth becomes an ambiguous topos that is relevant to life. The question arises as to how and where one stands toward the truth (as an overarching but world-effecting horizon of responsibility).[115]

Because ambiguities inevitably involve insecurities and uncertainties, "doubt" itself can become a structural element of human existence (Dasein), as Kierkegaard has shown in *Fear and Trembling* and *Sickness unto Death*.[116] Doubt also has a structurally positive element; from a theological point of view, doubt prevents man from allowing God to become an assumption and an idol who has become harmless to him. If man gives God a clear, unambiguous definition, God's potential to irritate is no longer permitted. Theologically, this can prove to be a positive because inner-worldly ambiguity is located in the dialectic of freedom and danger, without reaching a moment of force that would no longer allow for freedom. God, despite his revelation, grants freedom to man through his knowledge of God so that the relationship between God and man doesn't become coercive. God makes space available to man so that man can make positive choices about his own decisions and what is of existential significance to him. Thereby, the world becomes a topological opportunity, granted by God, to which one can declare one's fidelity without drifting off or becoming enmeshed in objectionable simplifications.[117] Faith, despite its fragility, can bear witness to its authenticity in this space for the profession of faith because it can be existentially relevant.

Badiou begins this section on the precariousness and fragility of faith with a passage from Paul: "But we have this treasure in clay jars, so that it may be made clear that this extraordinary power belongs to God and does not come from us" (2 Cor 4:7). However, the quality of doubt is noticeably lacking. As soon as one has decided in favor of the subjective gesture of decision that the event has in fact taken place, the question is no longer posed whether the event did in fact take place or whether Jesus Christ actually rose from the dead.[118] Just as there is

115. See Otmar Meuffels, "Der Mut, die Wahrheit beim Namen zu nennen: Gedanken zur Dogmatik," *MThZ* 64, no. 3 (2013): 255–56, 266–86.
116. See Kierkegaard, *Fear and Trembling*; and Søren Kierkegaard, *The Sickness unto Death: A Christian Exposition for Upbuilding and Awakening*, ed. and trans. Howard V. Hong and Edna H. Hong (Princeton, NJ: Princeton University Press, 1980).
117. See Ingolf U. Dalferth, "Religion und Wahrheit," in Dalferth and Stoellger, *Wahrheit in Perspektiven*, 195–232.
118. See Žižek, *Ticklish Subject*, 135–36, 138.

no impartial perspective, it seems like there is also no reversible perspective. As soon as the binary, categorical decision for the existence of the event has taken place, then the existence of the event seems unquestionable and irreversible because one commits oneself to continuous and decisive fidelity to the event.[119]

If one now takes what has been presented here as an object of critique and subjects it to reflections on its compatibility with theology, it is clear that the reflections about the event decision can be easily integrated into the concept of *fides qua*.[120] Yet this is a compromise in regard to the concept of *fides quae*. To be sure, Badiou begins with the theme of the generic horizon of the event and also touches on a subsequent possibility of logical deduction that emerges from the new evental horizon—although this turns out to be too weak to make a theological-doctrinal connection.[121] Badiou's reflections on the event emphasize the subjective decision of the event: the individual steps out from the universal, but this can also, strictly speaking, lead to him becoming isolated.

If one takes the theological foundations of Trinitarianism seriously, as related to both the act and the content of faith, then one must keep in mind that faith is not a separating or isolating event because the Holy Spirit—that is, the Spirit of Truth—stipulates, as a perspectival opening through grace, the possibility of an act of faith and an introduction into the content of the mystery of faith (John 16:13) by introducing the faithful to it (DV 4, 972–73). The Holy Spirit, in accordance with the Augustinian doctrine of the Trinity—with its special attention to the relational reality of God—is the binding bond of love between the loving father and his beloved son, who also accepts his love; the Holy Spirit also represents the unifying and binding bond between the faithful in the church (see *Lumen gentium* [LG] 7, 853) because, according to LG, the church itself is an icon of the Trinity (see LG 4, 851; *Unitatis redintegratio* [UR] 2, 908–9).[122] The inner-Trinitarian and the ecclesiastical,

119. See Badiou, *Saint Paul*, 90–91.
120. See Lothar Lies, "Fides qua—fides quae creditur," in *LThK*, vol. 3, cols. 1274–75.
121. See Badiou, *Being and Event*, 252, 397.
122. See Kehl, *Kirche*, 56, 66, 69, 74. See also Kehl:

> But there is simultaneously the other, more *epistemological* perspective, namely to view the Holy Spirit as the so-called "transcendental" *facilitator* of faith in Jesus Christ. One can only recognize *through* the Holy Spirit that the historical Jesus is really Christ, i.e. the event of God's self-revelation in person, and that the crucified man arose from the dead and was resurrected . . . ; if one does not specify the meeting place of the "Holy Spirit," where both God opened our eyes, as well as we ourselves, there can be no faith. Because only someone, who allows himself to be led into the loving relationship between Father and Son, into the Holy Spirit that binds them, can also be given the eyes of love, with which he can recognize the eternal Son of the Father in the historical Jesus. (69)

communio, are affected by the Holy Spirit. The communal-constitutive function of the Holy Spirit can be viewed from here, without difficulty, as an entry to an internal openness. Through the support of the Holy Spirit, the shibboleth distinction is opened so that one can begin from an internal plausibility and therefore also from an internal pneumatologically conditioned openness and a pneumatologically based discourse space;[123] to be sure, in reference to Badiou, this leads to a credible subjectivity, but it also keeps an enduring community element ready.[124] Here the individual believers, without denying them their dignity as subjects or persons, become bound together into a collective subject—the church: "So the church is the sheepfold, whose single necessary door is Christ" (LG 6, 851).

If one interprets faith as an existential acceptance of the support of the Holy Spirit, and as a gesture of decision in favor of the reality of the resurrection, then one of faith's defining characteristics is that it is based on the lasting truth procedure of a (public) declaration of truth.[125] According to Romans 10:9–10, "If you confess with your lips that Jesus is Lord and believe in your heart that God raised him from the dead, you will be saved. For one believes with the heart and so is justified, and one confesses with the mouth and so is saved."

To be sure, the Holy Spirit requires an individual's declaration of faith (1 Cor 12:3–4), but this is the same Holy Spirit who brings these subjects together into the confessional community of the church and unites them into one body with many members (1 Cor 12:12–27). In this way, individual and collective elements of faith will emerge from a common origin, through the Holy Spirit, and neither the subjective dignity of the individual will be infringed upon nor will the collective disintegrate into mere fragmentation because both elements remain connected to each other—not based on confrontation but by cooperating with each other.[126] The individual becomes a member of the community while retaining his subjectivity and self-worth, but in terms of function, he can assist in building the community (Eph 4:7–16).

123. See Bründl, *Nähe*, 128.
124. To be fair to Badiou, one must note that he points out, in one passage, that the church is the place for collective professions of faith and listening to the experience of the resurrection; this topic is then dropped from consideration and isn't mentioned again. See Badiou, *Saint Paul*, 99–106.
125. See Badiou, 88.
126. See Klauck, *1. Korintherbrief*: "The Holy Spirit doesn't only have an impact in one direction, that is, not only in highly ecstatic phenomena such as glossolalia; to the contrary, it provokes the most varied, in actuality, all manifestations of the Christian life of faith. In this regard, Paul is a champion of pluralism" (85).

The Bible as Holy Scripture

Alain Badiou offers a very compelling analysis of Saint Paul's claim that the decision to choose faith entails, in principle, a radically subjective element—that is, that faith becomes possible only through radical subjectivity. Nevertheless, there appears to be a certain amount of bias in Badiou's reading of Saint Paul. This becomes problematic if one asks the question, "How could one even come to the realization that the decision to choose faith is a radically subjective event for Paul?" given that we have only one source for Paul's perspective—his authentic letters.

These letters—and this is the decisive point—were meant for a public audience, that of the faithful (the early Christian community).[127] Their format alone gives this radical subjectivity a dialectical form in that the letters are addressed to a counterpart who already has faith through the subjective decision to accept grace. The description of this position occurs through language, and this counterpart is not an individual but rather a specifically targeted public audience. This dialectical form of radical subjectivity that is simultaneously conveyed to a counterpart also appears in Søren Kierkegaard's *Fear and Trembling*—a book whose pseudonymous dedication expresses something that is inexpressible; this is the reason Kierkegaard, the pseudonymous author of the work, specifies the name of the speaker, Johannes de Silentio.[128] The book treats this problem of how to convey radical, inexpressible subjectivity from the point of view of language; it spells this out in the Abraham narrative, specifically through Abraham's necessary silence toward Sarah and Isaac:

> This is the case with Abraham. He can say everything, but one thing he cannot say, and if he cannot say that—that is, say it in such a way that the other understands it—then he is not speaking. The relief provided by speaking is that it translates me into the universal. Now, Abraham can describe his love for Isaac in the most beautiful words to be found in any language. But this is not what is on his mind; it is something deeper, that he is going to sacrifice him because it is an ordeal. No one can understand the latter,

127. See Stefan Schreiber, "Briefliteratur im Neuen Testament," in Ebner and Schreiber, *Einleitung in das Neue Testament*, 255.
128. See Liessmann, *Sören Kierkegaard*, 58.

> and thus everyone can only misunderstand the former. The tragic hero does not know this distress. . . .
>
> The tragic hero does not know the dreadful responsibility of loneliness. Moreover, he has the consolation that he can weep and lament with Clytemnestra and Iphigenia—and tears and cries are relieving, but groanings that cannot be uttered are torturing. . . . This Abraham cannot do. . . . Speak he cannot; he speaks no human language. . . .
>
> At every moment, Abraham can stop; he can repent of the whole thing as a spiritual trial; then he can speak out, and everybody will be able to understand him—but then he is no longer Abraham.
>
> Abraham *cannot* speak, because he cannot say that which would explain everything (that is, so it is understandable): that it is an ordeal such that, please note, the ethical is the temptation. Anyone placed in such a position is an emigrant from the sphere of the universal.[129]

Kierkegaard considers Abraham—just as in Žižek's Kierkegaard rereading[130]—as a paradigm for the dialectical relationship between extreme subjectivity and universal mediation. Herein lies the paradox in Kierkegaard's project: the reappraisal of the problem of subjectivity can't take place outside the medium of the universal—that is, of language—and therefore not beyond the universal. Discourse about the termination of the universal can only take place within the universal and through the linguistic communication of the universal.[131] We know about Abraham and his inner conflict only through the linguistic presentation in the Bible; we are therefore strictly dependent on biblical transmission to gain any access to the enigma of Abraham's situation.

To be sure, Paul uses the idea that "faith comes from what is heard" (Rom 10:17); he expresses his resignation over the rejection of the universal message of salvation

129. Kierkegaard, *Fear and Trembling*, 113–15. See also Kierkegaard: "Abraham cannot be mediated; in other words, he cannot speak. As soon as I speak, I express the universal, and if I do not do so, no one can understand me" (60).
130. See Žižek, *Ticklish Subject*, 115.
131. A similar analysis still needs to be done for discourse about negative theology. Within theological speech, the inadequacy of theological language itself is only possible within the framework of the discourse of theological language—because otherwise, as Wittgenstein has clearly pointed out, one must be silent.

by the Israelites in a bitter tone of voice[132] even though access to faith through the mediation of a third party—that is, the prophets and the apostles—is still possible. We must nevertheless keep in mind that the mediating authority and the effect of grace that comes through faith (justice comes from faith) are not authorities that man has granted to himself. To the contrary, the christological dimension must also be demonstrated in the profession of faith. The New Testament scholar Ulrich Wilckens comments as follows on the authority of the act of proclamation in Romans 10:17: "Of course the more detailed definition of the word as the Word of Christ extends beyond verse 8 (i.e., Rom 10:8). Christ himself speaks and acts through the word of faith, just as God himself acts through the words of the prophets."[133]

The act of conveying the message of faith becomes a divine-human interactional event in which man, as the messenger, uses language to communicate the message of salvation to his counterpart. The effect of faith and—to speak in Pauline language—also justice has its foundation in God's acts; Wilckens notes that Christ himself becomes influential through his own words. The word of Christ gets its authority from within himself and not through human authority that man grants to himself; in other words, man can neither grant himself authority through the act of communicating the message of faith nor offer justification to a counterpart through the act of proclamation. Authority is always granted or mediated; it isn't subject to man's own sovereignty.[134] One can see here the ambiguity of the signifier in the concept of the "word of Christ." The word of Christ contains a *genitivus obiectivus* in that the proclamation of Jesus Christ is a statement with content, whereas here the dimension of authority, likewise of common origin, can be specified as a *genitivus subiectivus* because man does not grant validity, effectiveness, or even sanctity to the message of faith: this is based on divine action alone. The message of the proclamation, and also of the Bible, has a surplus *character* that can't simply be ascribed to human language as a pure medium of communication because this would undermine its divine dimension.

From this view, one can attribute an intentional surplus to the biblical text; this surplus can be ascribed to neither the intentionality of the author nor the reader's

132. See Ulrich Wilckens, *Der Brief an die Römer, Teilband 2, Römer 6–11* (Neukirchen-Vluyn, Germany: Neukirchener Verlag, 1987), 229–34.
133. Wilckens, 229.
134. The *Catechism of the Catholic Church* (CCC) therefore emphasizes the fact that a priest's authority is only granted by Christ (see Rom 10:17).

understanding because the biblical text reports of the *Deus semper maior*, who can also mediate his grace throughout the entire biblical text so that man attains justice and faith by hearing the message. The biblical text can't be reduced to human elements or components because that would ignore the pneumatological dimension of the text. The biblical text has its own purpose in which, using the analogy of the Symbolon of Chalcedon, the divine dimension exists in a simultaneous and inseparable relationship with the human dimension (among others, the finite signifier).[135]

In order to reappraise this tripartite structure hermeneutically, Umberto Eco's distinction is helpful; Eco rejects Roland Barthes's radical claim of the text's interpretive authority over the author's.[136] He declares that there is a categorial separation between the intention of the author (*intentio auctoris*) and the intention of the text—that is, of the work (*intentio operis*)—in which the intention of the reader (*intentio lectoris*) serves as the final component.[137] The text takes a middle position between the author and the reader in such a way that both never enter into direct communication with each other; to the contrary, the entity of the text itself, with its fixed arrangement of signifiers, is the determining factor in its reception. Authors create texts based on their own individual horizons of meaning and therefore produce their work with a particular intention, the *intentio auctoris*. The text is separate from the author's intention (the *intentio auctoris*); the text has its own self-determined horizon of meaning (*intentio operis*) that possesses its own enduring, excessive character. Neither the author nor the reader, each of whom has their own enduring perspective and their own enduring reading (*intentio lectoris*), can access it. The text creates its own effects through the (relative) uncontrollability of the words used in it.[138] To be sure, the text has a determined

135. See *DH*, 302. The Council of Chalcedon considered the natures of Jesus Christ and turned against radical positions by only addressing peripheral points regarding the natural relationship and by avoiding defining the mechanically precise interconnections. This created an integral space that was "without confusion or change, without division or separation" (DH, 302).

136. See Barthes, "Death," 142–43, 147–48.

137. See Umberto Eco, *The Limits of Interpretation* (Bloomington: Indiana University Press, 1990), 50–52. See also Jürgen Straub, *Handlung, Interpretation, Kritik: Grundzüge einer textwissenschaftlichen Handlungs- und Kulturpsychologie* (Berlin: De Gruyter, 1999), 227, 236–38.

138. See Umberto Eco, "Between Author and Text," in Umberto Eco, *Interpretation and Overinterpretation*, ed. Stefan Collini and with contributions by Richard Rorty, Jonathan Culler, and Christine Brooke-Rose (Cambridge: Cambridge University Press, 1992), 74. Eco, from his own point of view as an author, writes the following about the responses that a text has produced: "The text is there, and it produces its own effects. Whether I wanted it this way or not, we are now faced with a question, an ambiguous provocation; and I myself feel embarrassed in interpreting this conflict, though I realize a meaning lurks there (perhaps many meanings do)." Eco, 74.

structure of signifiers—which makes it, in this regard, finite—but the singularity and the ontic identity (Eigensein) of the work can never be conclusively deduced from the readerly act of reception. In this regard, the work possesses interminable dimensions that can be declared to be infinite. These unlimited dimensions in its hermeneutic reception led Eco, in an early work, to even speak of a work of art, in and of itself, as an enduring "open work of art" because it remains open to having the recipient give it a (constructed) meaningful response. In his later works, Eco focused more on the work itself and could thereby do greater justice to the singularity of the work by granting it the status of "quasi entity" and recognizing its intentional, distinctive content through the concept of "*intentio operis*." However, instead of opening the door to total interpretive freedom, according to Eco, it is nevertheless important to bear in mind the relatively transparent intention of the text and not succumb to capricious interpretive acrobatics.[139]

The text creates its own effects that can extend beyond the *intentio auctoris*; these can add an unintended connotation to the text that can be at odds with the author's actual intention—but the text has now been written, completed, and released for critical reception. The actual *intentio auctoris* is now only of limited relevance to its reception history, even if one considers that the contextualization of the author's actual intention has been—that is, can always be—influenced by unconscious and ambiguous, arbitrary factors.[140] Individual authors can't be asked about the wide horizon of literary works because the deliberate statement of intention of the real *intentio auctoris* toward fiction would seem weak. Eco is very clear about the role of the author's intention in its reception after the text was written, even when it comes to living authors: "But the text is there, and the empirical author has to remain silent."[141]

This discussion of the hermeneutic conditions for establishing the one and only correct authorial intention—that this is a phantom and a fiction because even authors aren't conscious of the clarity of their intentions—is also applicable, to an even greater extent, in determining the possible intentions of authors of the Bible. Not only did these authors bring their own themes and theories together in

139. See Eco, "Author," 78. See Straub, *Handlung*: "Eco doesn't think much of those so-called 'experts' who deliberately present misleading interpretations of a text, by covering up what's actually in the text through their own subtle and illustrious, or rough and bizarre readings" (231).
140. See Straub, *Handlung*, 247–49.
141. Eco, "Author," 79.

a narrative form, but these authors relied on previously written traditional materials (such as the Q source for Matthew and Luke) and integrated them into their biblical work, and/or they participated in a discourse of a time period that is only accessible to us with great effort. Examples include the sources of the Babylonian and Neo-Assyrian creation myths in Genesis or the Gospel's concept of Roman divinization of the state and emperor in the Gospel according to Mark.[142]

We can't ask the authors of the Bible themselves about their discursive backgrounds because many questions would entail some reasoning that wouldn't be valid to biblical interpreters: for example, if one were to ask the author of the Gospel according to Matthew about the use of the Trinitarian baptismal formula (Matt 28:19) and its theological implications, the author's answer would likely appear as insufficient.[143] Such a line of inquiry would undermine the authority of the biblical texts because the human side of biblical literary production can be, and is, only ascertained here. The authority of Holy Scripture doesn't derive from the fact that it is a collection of the most influential books of Judeo-Christian culture; rather, Vatican II states clearly that the authority of Holy Scripture derives from the fact that it was "written under the influence of the Holy Spirit" (DV 11, 975). The inspiration for Holy Scripture stipulates that it has authority within the church and isn't only viewed as a book whose themes and motifs have authoritatively influenced the Western cultural horizon.[144] The inspiration for the books of Holy Scripture, by the Holy Spirit, is also the reason these books "teach firmly, faithfully and without error such truth as God, for the sake of our salvation, wished the biblical text to contain" (DV 11, 976). In this way, the books of Holy Scripture participate in the divine infallibility and truth that are beyond the specifications set down in writing.[145]

It is totally alien to the council to claim a naturalistic inerrancy of Holy Scripture; to the contrary, the historicity of the New Testament gospels is clearly stated (DV 19, 978). Therefore, individual errors in Holy Scripture (e.g., dates,

142. See Dorothea Sattler and Theodor Schneider, "C. Schöpfungslehre," in Schneider, *Handbuch der Dogmatik*, 1:125–35. See also Martin Ebner, "B. V. Das Markus-evangelium," in Ebner and Schreiber, *Einleitung in das Neue Testament*, 175–80.
143. Similarly, Vatican II also focuses on Holy Scripture and not on the hagiographer (with the exception of DV 12, 976). In DV 12 (976), there is a warning that one must keep in mind the intention of the hagiographer and be aware that while reading a passage, it is the aim of the exegete to work toward a deeper meaning of Holy Scripture so that the church can gain a deeper understanding of Holy Scripture.
144. See Hoping, "Theologischer Kommentar," 766.
145. See Hoping, 770.

official titles, or similar things) don't present problems for the inspiration of Holy Scripture because the council didn't exploit the biblical authors by degrading them and referring to them as God's writing tools[146]—otherwise, one would encounter the complex of problems of biblical inspiration. Instead, the council viewed the composition of Scripture as an event of divine-human interaction; the equal participation of both partners is clearly expressed by designating them both as *auctores* (DV 11, 975–76).[147] Furthermore, the text of the council declares that the authors are true authors, *veri auctores*, whose full humanity is unapologetically emphasized in their individual "abilities and strengths"; this allows for human error and inaccuracies because these can persist without affecting God's truth of salvation (DV 11, 975–76). Because God's mystery of salvation is something that human understanding can never fully fathom through reason but is relevant to man and his life, it nonetheless pleased God to appear to man through self-revelation for the sake of salvation (DV 6, 973).

A person of faith doesn't directly encounter a written description of God's will for salvation in Holy Scripture; rather, human words were used in the divine-human interaction of this transcription so that human and divine intention has been distilled in this event of interaction (DV 12, 976). This implies that historical-critical exegesis is fully justified when dealing with theological hermeneutics and in researching the divine mystery of salvation (DV 12, 976). The biblical text is not an exhaustive, written transmission of divine truth, but it participates in it through inspiration, and as a witness, it refers to the continuously expanding greatness of God.[148]

In order to prevent a possibly erroneous interpretation of the relevance of salvation in the biblical text, Vatican II states (DV 13, 977) that the focus of divine revelation is on God's self-communication in the incarnation of Jesus Christ and not on didactically determining theoretical divine instructions in human words. Revelation occurred for the sake of man's salvation, whereas in Holy Scripture, the

146. See Hoping, 767, 708.
147. Nevertheless, it is recommended that one not translate *auctores* to "author" because this would imply a double authority problem. One clearly does greater justice to the event of interaction, and one avoids the deconstructionist author discourse, by equating the divine part with original authorship and the human part with derived authorship, just as was done in the translations of *HThK*, *Vatican II*, and Rahner's and Vorgrimler's compendium of councils. See Karl Rahner and Herbert Vorgrimler, *Kleines Konzilskompendium: Sämtliche Texte des Zweiten Vatikanums* (Freiburg, Germany: Herder, 1980), 373.
148. See Hoping, "Kommentar," 772–73.

focus is on a "wonderful *condescension* of eternal wisdom."[149] There is an analogy between the incarnation of Jesus Christ and the word of Holy Scripture—as in the earlier reference to the Symbolon of Chalcedon—in which a similarity is expressed. The word of Holy Scripture conveys a premonition and a preview of God's greatness and magnificence that appears to man through God's self-revelation. An analogy requires that a similarity exists between at least two (or more) factors in certain but not all aspects.[150]

The analogy between the word of Holy Scripture and God's incarnate Word necessitates, in a negative way, a radical différance due to their unbridgeable qualitative difference: divine truth can never be identical to the written word of the Bible because "the limitation of the human word . . . is never fully [able] to express God's mysteries."[151] One fails to appreciate the personal dimension of God's devotion to man's salvation if one ties this devotion to an inalterable precision and accuracy in the biblical text that is far removed from the time period. God's eternal will for salvation for all of creation, and particularly for humanity, emerges in a personal event of encounter between Jesus Christ and humanity so that Jesus Christ himself validates the actual source of revelation. Rudolf Voderholzer uses this as an opportunity to differentiate the Christian understanding of revelation that follows the *Dogmatic Constitution on Divine Revelation*, DV, from an Islamic understanding of revelation: "As a person, Christ is the only source of revelation in the strict sense of the word. The decisive insight that follows from this is that Holy Scripture is not in essence direct self-revelation, but that Holy Scripture, as the book of the Church, is proof of revelation. Christianity, if one is to even use the term 'religion,' is not a religion of the book, and not the Biblical religion, but rather the religion of Jesus Christ."[152]

149. The council text on the theme of condescension refers to John Chrysostom, the theologian of late antiquity; the general neo-Platonic horizon of understanding of late antiquity implies echoes of Neoplatonism. Divine truth, in and of itself, can therefore never find its complete form of realization in finite conditions. There is a radical, unbridgeable qualitative difference between the greatness and eternity of God and all other secondary, existing factors, although through the realities that participate in divine truth and magnificence, there can be reference to God's greatness and magnificence.
150. See Hans Jörg Sandkühler, "Analogie," in *Enzyklopädie Philosophie*, vol. 1, A–N (Hamburg, Germany: Meiner, 1999), 47–48.
151. Hoping, "Kommentar," 776. Thus it doesn't have a negative impact on the text as a testimonial of the truth of salvation if human errors or inaccuracies are found in it, because the content of the revelation isn't that of supernatural statements of faith but is better defined as a personal encounter between God and man and the fulfilling of God's self-revelation in the process.
152. Rudolf Voderholzer, *Offenbarung, Tradition und Schriftauslegung: Bausteine zu einer christlichen Bibelhermeneutik* (Regensburg, Germany: F. Pustet, 2013), 54–55.

That fact that God communicates through Jesus Christ ensures that the message and the messenger are identical in Jesus Christ and that they merge into one person.[153] The message of the kingdom of God, its unfolding, and finally the encounter there with God culminate in Jesus Christ. He is the primary focus of the self-revealing event of revelation that reaches its peak in him (DV 4, 972): The Old Testament pattern of promise and future fulfillment is disrupted because there can't be any higher fulfillment of God's promise than for God to show himself directly to man. Therefore, biblical Scripture can't be revelation itself; yet the council recognizes that one can find the principal testimony of the words and deeds of Christ in the gospels and that this testimony has special authority because the gospels are pneumatologically inspired (DV 18, 978). They are therefore subsequent to the actual event of revelation; this explains why Holy Scripture and tradition are tied together in DV 9 (974–75), but they aren't identical as well. Holy Scripture takes precedence over tradition because transmission only becomes possible through Holy Scripture.[154] In DV 9 (974–75), several theological perspectives intersect that preferably should all get a hearing based on their legitimate authority; the text begins by tying Scripture and its transmission together in order to give Scripture precedence over transmission because tradition "only" passes on God's entrusted, unaltered word. However, it is emphasized in the concluding sentence that Scripture and tradition are to be equally honored.[155]

The question of how to determine the authority of both of these elements is not entirely clarified in the council text because a pneumatological dimension is attributed to both of them. Holy Scripture is inspired by the divine and has God as its originator (DV 11, 975), whereas tradition brings progress and thereby also an increased understanding of faith because the Holy Spirit accompanies the church and always leads people of faith deeper into God's truth (DV 8, 974). The question of material sufficiency and insufficiency couldn't be answered by the council text because there were conflicts among the council fathers in their discussions of this exact question.[156]

153. See Voderholzer, 54.
154. Thus Cardinal Florit, in a preparation text for session 3 of the Second Vatican Council, notes this: tradition doesn't emerge before Holy Scripture, which then makes initial interpretations possible. See Hoping, "Kommentar," 760.
155. See Hoping, 759–61.
156. See Hoping, 751.

The decisive factor is that there is only one source of revelation: God's self-revelation through the incarnation event of divine Logos.[157] In the kenosis of God, God's love and his love of man are demonstrated to man. Although this love is not immediately apparent and plausible to man, from an external perspective, this event of revelation and renunciation can appear as foolishness (1 Cor 1:18–25). In order to be able to believe that the unparalleled truth of salvation is demonstrated to man in the words and deeds of Jesus Christ and that Jesus Christ himself is "the way, and the truth, and the life" (John 14:6), one needs the support of the Holy Spirit, who makes the perspective of faith possible in the first place. Only through faith does the Bible become Holy Scripture and Jesus of Nazareth become the promised Christ, only through faith does the history of the church become a pilgrimage for God's people, and only through faith does the tradition of the church become an ever-deepening understanding of the divine truth of salvation.

God's self-revelation in Jesus Christ has attained a standard in human history that is fundamentally different from all previously enacted revelations communicated to man. Previously, God revealed himself through the prophets or in other mediated ways, but in the miraculous incarnation of his Eternal Son, God presents himself to man in a direct but humanly mediated presence that doesn't in any way revoke the mystery and the greatness of God's being (DV 2, 972; DV 4, 972; DV 6, 973). The relationship between God and man culminates in Jesus Christ because here God gives to man himself the knowledge of God's love and his eternal plan of salvation in order "to live among them and to tell them about the inner life of God" (DV 4, 972). This is the most intimate and qualitatively most intense encounter between God and man in history. Therefore, the council proclaims that this self-revelation surpasses all previous revelation so "that no new public revelation is to be expected before the glorious manifestation of our lord Jesus Christ" (DV 4, 973).

Man encounters God in an unmediated but humanly mediated way; this creates an insurmountable task for man because in the interests of divine salvation, man is granted a share in "those divine treasures which totally surpass human

157. In the preparation text *De fontibus revelationes*, misleading wording referring to two sources of revelation was still being used; subsequently, it was the concern of the majority of the council to prove that the only source of revelation was God (DV 9, 974). See Hoping, 720–32.

understanding" (DV 6, 973).[158] If one expresses this encounter between God and man in Jacques Lacan's terminology, one would say that man encounters the Real in Jesus Christ's self-revelation. Because the Real is incomprehensible, unrecognizable, and unbearable for man (hence God's warning to Moses not to look at his face because nobody comes through this alive [Exod 33:20]), the Real appears in a humanly mediated form—in a symbolic form that is closely connected to the Real. Man acquires the perspective of faith through the Holy Spirit's gift of grace, and he recognizes that he has encountered the Real, but he has to translate this in a symbolic way so that he can somehow manage it. The Emmaus disciples acted in this way; they compared their interpretations when they encountered the Real—the resurrected Christ—and subsequently translated this event into the realm of the Symbolic so that they would be able to comprehend it.[159] Because the Real appears in Jesus Christ through symbolic mediation and, furthermore, is even revealed (although faith is essential for this to happen), one can risk making the conceptual leap and—to use Lacan's vocabulary—refer to Jesus Christ as the symbol of the Real.[160] The message and the person are inextricably intertwined so that the divine proclamation of the coming of the kingdom of God at the end of time can only be announced by Jesus Christ. This message of salvation, of the final unfolding of God's love for his creation, also couldn't be corrupted by man's absolute rejection of the crucifixion of Jesus Christ. Faith is a gift from God to man that is founded on grace and can be rejected by man. Christ's crucifixion is the ultimate expression of God's love, a love that isn't forced but heals.

For Lacan, the intruding and incomprehensible Absolute is the Real itself, and it is incomprehensible and always unintelligible to man; in contrast, through the incarnation of Christ's life, works, and resurrection, a decidedly Christian understanding

158. Vatican II cites the "Dogmatic Constitution on the Catholic Faith, *Dei Filius*" of Vatican I (chap. 2, "On Revelation," 2:806) here; see also *DH*, 3005. *Dei Filius* refers to 1 Corinthians 2:9 to describe the quality of divine revelation as a contrast to man's natural condition: "What no eye has seen, nor ear heard, nor the human heart conceived, what God has prepared for those who love him."

159. It should not be a problem for this investigation that the third category of the Borromean knot, the Imaginary, has been given little attention. It is up to the reader to determine its relevance for self-revelation. Perhaps one should think here of the theologumenon of the *visio beatifica*. See Gisbert Greshake, "Visio beatifica," in *LThK*, vol. 10, col. 810.

160. According to Karl-Heinz Menke, symbolic reality, described as abstractly as possible, is "a symbol, to whose self-actualization the expressed reality belongs. . . . Symbolic reality mustn't be separated from the reality that it describes, although it is very different from it. In other words, symbolic reality is tied to symbolized reality, in that it can only reach completion through it." See "Realsymbol," in *LThK*, vol. 8, cols. 867–68.

of revelation differs significantly from the Lacanian Real. Through the incarnation of Jesus Christ, God wants to communicate a message that is understandable to man, or to use Lacan's language, he wants to communicate a symbolic message of the intrusion and dawning of God's eschatological reign. However, in order to share this message with man and communicate it with authoritative validity, God chooses to communicate it through a human figure. The connection of both elements (true God and true man) with each other can't be undone;[161] this is neither an apparent nor a time-bound relationship against Docetism or modalism. Karl Rahner wanted to make it possible to describe this connection by using the concept of symbolic reality.[162] Even though the concept that Rahner introduced into theological discourse doesn't have a Lacanian semantic and it is difficult to harmonize the concept of symbolic reality with Lacan's concept of the Real,[163] given the approach of this investigation, it doesn't seem far-fetched—it even seems fitting—to preserve the concept of symbolic reality in its linguistic superficiality but also to simultaneously fit it into the horizon of Lacan's semantics.[164] Jesus Christ is the symbolic reality of God because it is here that God, as the unconditional and Absolute, intrudes directly into the world of humans, but not in an unmediated way, and in human form. Thus there is no tension in the dialectic of symbolic reality between overly rational—that is, divine truth—and humanly comprehensible communication; both elements—the incomprehensible as well as the comprehensible—are closely linked together and should neither be separated nor be mixed together (*DH*, 302):

> In the New Testament, the contemporary unveiling of a fact that has been hidden, occurred primarily through the communication of knowledge that was a testimony to God's will for salvation and was supposed to serve man's salvation, and therefore became the doctrine of salvation. Because in the New Testament, too, the devotion of our holy and merciful God wasn't so much directed towards irrational paths of enthusiasm and intuition . . . it

161. See DH, 302.
162. See Karl Rahner, "The Theology of the Symbol," in *Theological Investigations*, vol. 4, *More Recent Writings*, trans. Kevin Smyth (Baltimore: Helicon, 1966), 234–44.
163. The overlapping with the Real is very limited due to the (at least, to some degree) intellectually transparent horizon of the message of the kingdom of God.
164. According to Rahner, this is not an attempt to offer a *better* explanation of the concept of symbolic reality; the concern is much more to offer a *different* explanation, one that seeks to be in conversation with contemporary philosophy.

> initially took place along the clear paths of divine guidance, from Christ's mouth to the ear of the listener in the guise of understandable words and truths that could be passed down. Only then will the following statement be meaningful: "Revelation, in a narrow sense, has a specific content that can be recognized, and is accessible in hindsight." In other words, Christianity is both grace and truth (Jn 1:17).[165]

Jesus's message of the emergence of the kingdom of God is tied exclusively to his person, and the message is conveyed to man through the symbolic dimension of human speech. This message is not limited to the intellectual aspects of linguistic statements. Jesus's message calls for an additional existential transformation through its practical ethics; this is supposed to serve man as an example of a successful life that is suitable to the newly redeemed creation and newly redeemed man. Through God's unparalleled act of salvation, humanity (Menschsein) gains new qualities through redemption: the humanity (Menschsein) of the former Adam is transferred to the new Adam (Rom 5:12–22). In Hegelian fashion, this can be understood as a threefold sublation (Aufhebung): First, the mode of Being (Seinsweise) of the former Adam is "canceled" and thereby remembered. This mode of being doesn't get lost because it is preserved in memory. Second, the mode of being of the former Adam is "canceled" through Christ's deed and transferred to the new reality of creation so that the status (broken by sin) of the former Adam is canceled and annulled. And third, the humanity (Menschsein) of the former Adam is raised to a higher level and thereby brought into a more complete form and thereby "sublated" to a new level.[166] Christ is the new Adam because man finds a new form of being (Seinsform) in him as the creator and principle of all things (John 1:3–5).[167]

Through the symbolic reality of Jesus Christ, it is possible to direct man to his own destination in true human beingness (Menschsein) as the new Adam (*Gaudium*

165. Georg Söll, *Das Dasein im Glauben*, vol. 1/5, *Dogma und Dogmenentwicklung* (Freiburg, Germany: Herder, 1971), 27–28. It is important to note here that God's revelation is directly presented but isn't forced. To the contrary, it invites you to decide and follow it so that it will subsequently be explicitly recognized as divine truth. This comes to light very clearly in the distinction between pre-Easter, implied Christology, and explicit post-Easter Christology.
166. See Medard Kehl, *Eschatologie* (Würzburg, Germany: Echter Verlag, 1986), 91–94.
167. Irenaeus of Lyon expresses the idea in the *recapitulatio*—that is, ἀνακεφαλαιώσασις—that Christ is the head of creation and that creation is defined by him and transferred to a new form of Being (Seinsform) in him. See Ysabel de Andia, *Homo vivens: Incorruptibilité et divinisation de l'homme selon Irénée de Lyon* (Paris: Études Augustiniennes, 1986).

et spes [GS] 22, 1081) so that through symbolic reality, the imaginary dimension of his human existence is brought to his attention. Lacan sees the dimension of the Imaginary in man's self-alienation and likewise in the desire of the other: "In short, nowhere does it appear more clearly that man's desire finds its meaning in the other's desire, not so much because the other holds the keys to the desired object, as because his first object(ive) is to be recognized by the other."[168]

Paul also recognizes the inner conflict—that is, man's alienation from himself and his own creative destination:[169] "For I do not do what I want, but I do the very thing I hate" (Rom 7:15). However, the decisive aspect of Pauline anthropology is not man's condition per se—that he is broken by sin; the focus is on overcoming his condition through Jesus Christ's act of redemption.

Just as I used the threefold sublation (Aufhebung) of the Hegelian mode of thinking to address the transition from the former Adam to the new Adam a bit earlier, the law was likewise "sublated" so that the new Adam also reaches a new, liberated basis for existence. The former Adam won't be forgotten; to the contrary, he continues to remain in force despite Christ's death for our salvation because Christ presents God's love of the world. This is taken to a new level so that Paul can say to the Roman parish, "For the one who loves another has fulfilled the law. . . . And any other commandment, are summed up in this word, 'Love your neighbor as yourself.' Love does no wrong to a neighbor; therefore, love is the fulfilling of the law" (Rom 13:8–10; see also Matt 5:17–19). Christ's death on the cross doesn't entail any automatism and thus doesn't force man to act out of grace. Man has been freed to act responsibly and reflectively so that he can do justice to his new status as a freed Being (Befreit-Seins; Rom 6:1–14).

Christ's death on the cross—as a this-worldly fact of human reason, it appears as foolishness (1 Cor 1:18–25)—frees human reason in the dimension of the kingdom of God so that it is no longer dependent on everyday occurrences or human inadequacies; human reason can now be a support for putting all one's hope in God and fulfilling the commandment of love (Matt 6:24–35; 22:34–40) without denouncing

168. Lacan, *Écrits*, 222.
169. See Wilckens, *Römer*: "Contradiction and misery therefore result in the alienation of the ego from its creaturely 'authenticity,' and the more hopeless the condition of the ego appears, the clearer it becomes that the ego, in its alienation, is a *salvandus*. Man's original condition as a creature is evident in his last words—in his call to his Savior (Rom 7:24)" (94).

human reason in the process.[170] Through his personal self-revelation, God intrudes into man's present day and proclaims, with exclusive authority and sovereignty, the emergence of the final kingdom of God, which leads man to the guiding principle to also follow God's love in one's own life in order to attain full human beingness (Menschsein; GS 22, 1081–82).[171]

It is fitting to introduce Lacan's three orders (Real, Symbolic, Imaginary) as a tool to explain Christ's incarnation and its meaning for man. The Real (God is directly in man's reality), the Symbolic (the message of the kingdom of God at the end of God's eschatological reign), and the Imaginary (the aspect of human perfection) culminate in Jesus Christ, according to a Christian understanding.

If one assumes an anthropology that is based on teleology, wherein man always wants to know and understand more, including things concerning faith (*credo, ut intelligam*), this thirst for knowledge can be viewed as an attempt to continuously transform the Real into the Symbolic, the order that man can understand; this an infinite, never-ending process.[172]

God's self-representation (in Jesus Christ) can never be adequately rendered in human words (as is the case for the gospels or the New Testament Epistles) because the eternal and divine always transcend the contingent and the created.[173] They

170. This is especially clear in the antitheses in the Sermon on the Mount. See Ulrich Luz, *Matthew 1–7: A Commentary*, trans. Wilhelm C. Linss (Minneapolis: Augsburg Fortress, 1989), 215–16. See also Stephan Ernst, *Grundfragen theologischer Ethik: Eine Einführung* (Munich, Germany: Kösel, 2009), 85–87.
171. See Hans-Joachim Sander, "Theologischer Kommentar zur Pastoralkonstitution über die Kirche in der Welt von heute, *Gaudium et spes*," in *HThK*, vol. 4:

> The first sentence [GS 22, 1081] contains the key statement: Christ's presence among people is an act of enlightenment: "vere clarescit" (it's truly clear). Christ answers the initial question of the entire chapter, "Who is man?" However, this doesn't happen in such a way that man is told that he will find fulfillment in Christ. Man is not subordinate to Christ; to the contrary, the mystery of "the Word incarnate," i.e., Christ as the site of God's incarnation, is attributed to man. There is a direct connection between who Christ is, and how man can become enlightened about himself. (739)

172. See Marion, *God without Being*, 139–44. The process of hermeneutic understanding always involves the condition that one will apply one's understanding of the meaning of the text to one's own life. An openness to the text can't arise until one accepts the desire to understand—an openness that doesn't set barriers a priori to the text due to the reader's stance. See Gadamer, *Truth and Method*, 404–5. Whatever is valid for the text itself is equally valid for the symbolic reality of the incarnation.
173. See Schmaus, *GdK*, vol. 1/1, 82. It is therefore evident from the God-man *différance* "that man is not in a position to adequately repeat the Word of God, that has been partially imparted to him. Because the inexpressible mystery, that is God, is in each of God's actions and can therefore not be fully captured in human concepts or words. Even the announcement of the bearer of revelation has the character of *theologia negativa*." Schmaus, 82.

are a hint or a trace, and man is only offered a notion of God's greatness[174] when he sees "the eternal wisdom stoop down" (DV 13, 977), but he can never integrate God's abundance: *Deus semper maior.*[175] Man continuously attempts to make God more understandable and comprehensible to himself, although this is impossible through an autonomous authority over language (man neither has this authority nor is able to understand God's Being [Sein Gottes]). Man can only understand God to the extent that God himself makes it possible for man to understand him—because insight into matters of faith itself needs God's grace.

To be sure, man performs this act of verbalization and textualization in the manner of a secondary cause; however, God himself gives precedence to the primary cause of this attempt by the gift of grace through the Holy Spirit himself because he sends the Holy Spirit as a guide who leads ever deeper to the truth (DV 8, 974). The person who acts as if he were all-powerful in his attempt to fathom the mystery of God denies the grace of the Holy Spirit and doesn't recognize God; he only recognizes his own idol.[176]

The Hermeneutics of Doctrine within Human Time

The leap of faith requires a radical subjectivity that is linked to a content-related issue, even if only secondarily. The content-related dimension is connected to its communicative and social context, whose meaning is conditioned by the Other. Because experiences with God and his traces in the world are ambiguous, they can only be understood if they are viewed within their social context.[177] From an ecclesiological view, this radical subjectivity can lead to a solipsistic way of thinking; it therefore can't be considered a structural site for today's experience of

174. See Meuffels, Gott, 135. See Derrida, *Writing and Difference*, 67–76, 174–85. See also Derrida, *On the Name*. God's revelation stays open for interpretation without falling into the postmodern situation of a "holding pattern" and an insatiable longing because Christianity is specifically characterized by professing one's allegiance to a positive revelation. See also Magnus Striet, *In der Gottesschleife: Von religiöser Sehnsucht in der Moderne* (Freiburg, Germany: Herder, 2014), 31, 53.
175. Holy Scripture has a pneumatological intentionality that can never be fully accessed; to the contrary, it always points to the larger mystery of God—it is an indication and testimony of God's self-revelation and can, through its pneumatological dimension, become an icon. Holy Scripture doesn't have strict evidentiary standards—it mustn't have them—because it would become static: "The witness doesn't prove what he has witnessed. But he can invite one to engage with it and experience experiences with it that it communicates." See Jürgen Werbick, "Die Autorität der Zeugen—und andere Glaubwürdigkeiten: Ein ekklesiologischer Diskurs über die Glaubwürdigkeit," in *Glaube in Gemeinschaft: Autorität und Rezeption in der Kirche*, ed. Markus Knapp and Thomas Söding (Freiburg, Germany: Herder, 2014), 25.
176. See Marion, *God*, 29–33.
177. See Meuffels, Gott, 42, 51.

God.[178] The self-revelation of Jesus Christ should be primarily understood not as an instructional, theoretical message about norms and commandments but rather as a direct, personal, communicative encounter between God and man within human time. Because God entered human time to reveal himself to man with his message of salvation, Jesus Christ himself became an irrevocable part of human history; therefore, human history is the site of faith and, as such, must also be reappraised.[179]

God offers himself to man through his welcoming love. In order to understand this dimension of Jesus's message of the kingdom of God, the Easter event and subsequent reflection on it were necessary within the narrative and interpretive community of the church (Luke 24:13–35).[180] The New Testament does not offer a truly cogent, evidence-based, unambiguous interpretation of the Easter event, with its soteriological implications, that would bring a sense of closure to the matter. To the contrary, it offers a wide range of perspectives.

Christianity's search for knowledge didn't end with the texts included in the New Testament; rather, it found its initial and normative foundation here. Professions of faith in the New Testament haven't been lost over time; they remain part of the tradition. They represent the authoritative and normative material foundation for further efforts at reflection that, in and of themselves, indicate further hermeneutic and epistemological progress in the development of professions of faith. If one considers this issue of the christological dimension, then one can recognize theological epistemological progress alone in the wide-ranging titles of highness conferred upon Jesus, including his divinity; in the earliest traces of Christian professions of faith, his titles indicated lower status (Rom 10:9: "Jesus is Lord"; likewise, 1 Cor 1:10). In the Gospel according to John, a universal dimension is attributed to Jesus's divinity through which he, as the principle for constituting Being (seinskonstituierende Prinzip), is acknowledged as having the same divine dignity as the Father

178. This does not mean that experiences of God are impossible outside of the church; nevertheless, through its sacramental structure, the church is a designated place for encountering God (LG 7, 854).

179. See Johannes Feiner, "Offenbarung und Kirche—Kirche und Offenbarung," in *Mysterium Salutis: Grundriss heilsgeschichtlicher Dogmatik*, vol. 1, *Die Grundlagen heilsgeschichtlicher Dogmatik*, ed. Johannes Feiner and Magnus Löhrer (Einsiedeln, Switzerland: Benziger Verlag, 1965), 511. It is therefore a matter of reexamining the time period of the church between Jesus's resurrection and his final appearance ("the Return") as the time of an encounter between God and man in which the past as memory and Christ's Word as an ongoing new encounter and actualization of his presence take place. Ecclesiastical time preserves its sacramental dimension through this structure.

180. See Meuffels, *Gott*, 55–59.

("In the beginning was the Word, and the Word was with God, and the Word was God. . . . All things came into being through him, and without him not one thing came into being" [John 1:1–3]). Likewise, "I am the way, and the truth, and the life. No one comes to the Father except through me" (John 14:6). Normative statements take place within the biblical tradition of theological conceptualizing. Normativity does not emerge only from the church's councils: "The formation of symbola doesn't only go back to the New Testament; it doesn't first appear on the 'margins of the canon.' It was there from the very beginning; at the very least, it's older than all New Testament writings. . . . Exegesis of the New Testament is increasingly viewed as a larger, though multi-layered traditional process, in which the original kerygma is continuously being updated and reinterpreted. When all is said and done, this traditional process extends beyond the time period of the canon to the period of the post-Apostolic Church. The Gospel and doctrine were never opposites."[181]

Because man's knowledge of God doesn't happen instantaneously but is rather a learning process that advances over time, one can't claim that there is hostility between Holy Scripture and tradition. The Bible itself is testimony of the earliest tradition of Christianity (which has its own process of tradition) and therefore has tradition as a condition of its own existence. Yet even tradition is tied to the Bible so that it doesn't stray too far from all-too-human perspectives and attempts for answers along its path to knowledge. Therefore, tradition considers the Bible, through its pneumatological authority, a definitive standard and corrective. The New Testament was able to be set down in writing, specified, and recognized as the canon because faith takes place in time, and it reaches deeper knowledge about Jesus Christ's self-revelation (within history) through a process of transmission that spans generations. Tradition was able to build and transmit a common body of religious belief that wouldn't get lost in fantastical descriptions that had no connection to the real life of Jesus Christ and would therefore have degenerated into phantasms. The biblical canon has a material basis that constantly warns faith, as a guiding principle, not to overestimate one's own capacity of interpretation. The biblical text refers, therefore, to Jesus Christ's *revelation* and becomes thereby the definitive *testimony* of revelation: "The text isn't the Gospel; to the contrary, it is a trustworthy witness of the Gospel."[182]

181. Kasper, *Dogma*, 76.
182. Kasper, 111.

The subsequent history of doctrine offers elegant testimony to the fact that biblical Scripture has not brought an end to man's questions about Christ's essence or his struggle to understand the meaning of Christ's death on the cross. Because Scripture occasionally entails ambiguities that are open to varying interpretations—both orthodox and heterodox[183]—it was a concern in the patristics not only that Scripture be properly understood but also that later developments in the church not be undertaken as a way to surpass and invalidate Scripture. Rather, one needed to adhere to the specifics of the witnesses in Scripture. Continuity with the source and the tradition associated with it were considered a guarantee of orthodoxy, whereas the loss of tradition—that is, abandoning tradition—went along with heresy: "The heretic came across as a person without tradition, precisely because of his opposition to traditional teachings. And if—unlike the Church—he couldn't trace a lineage for his ideas and a line of ancestors of like-minded people as far back as those who were likewise cited in the Bible, then the following verdict was handed down concerning his project: Nihil innovetur, nisi quod traditum est!"[184]

Ambiguity can't be overcome through tradition alone; because it requires deeper interpretation, the early church community was committed to seeking agreement in their interpretations. This would prevent the community from being torn apart by different perspectives or breaking apart. Above all, it would prevent Scripture from succumbing to wild interpretations by individuals.[185] This commitment is reflected

183. See Augustine, "Letter #120," in *The Works of Saint Augustine: A Translation for the 21st Century*, vol. 2/2, *Letters* 100–155 (*Epistulae*), ed. Boniface Ramsey, trans. Roland Teske (Hyde Park, NY: New City Press, 2003), 136.

184. Söll, *Das Dasein im Glauben*, 1/5:71–72.

185. See Vincent of Lérins, *The Commonitory of Vincent of Lérins, for the Antiquity and Universality of the Catholic Faith against the Profane Novelties of All Heresies*, in *Nicene and Post-Nicene Fathers*, 2nd ser., ed. Philip Schaff and Henry Wace, trans. C. A. Heurtley (Peabody, MA: Hendrickson, 1994), 11:132 (2, 1–2). Vincent of Lérins emphasizes the importance of taking tradition into account when interpreting Holy Scripture because Holy Scripture is first and foremost *the writing of the church* and must therefore be understood together with the apostolic manuscripts:

> But here someone perhaps will ask, Since the canon of Scripture is complete, and sufficient of itself for everything, and more than sufficient, what need is there to join with it the authority of the Church's interpretation? For this reason,—because, owing to the depth of Holy Scripture, all do not accept it in one and the same sense, but one understands its words in one way, another in another; so that it seems to be capable of as many interpretations as there are interpreters. For Novatian expounds it one way, Sabellius another, Donatus another, Arius, Eunomius, Macedonius, another, Photinus, Apollinaris, Priscillian, another, Iovanian, Pelagius, Celestius, another, lastly, Nestorius. Therefore, it is very necessary, on account of so great intricacies of such various error, that the rule for the right understanding of the prophets and apostles should be framed in accordance with the standard of Ecclesiastical and Catholic interpretation.

Vincent, 11:132 (2, 1–2).

in their constant efforts to reach consensus on the question of the doctrinal content of Christian faith. This process didn't go smoothly in all sorts of ways, which led to repeated squabbles and disputes that could only be overcome through collective struggles in their attempts to find answers and reach consensus. The Councils of Nicaea and Chalcedon are examples of these struggles.

As a starting point, one can see, in both examples, an excessive claim in an individual's answer to the question of the essence and relevance of Christ. Man misjudges the limits of his own interpretive authority and attempts to use human categories to make Christ's essence and the mystery of God's self-revelation comprehensible and manageable and also, to a certain extent, accessible to human reason.

Arius's concern was to limit the proliferation of mediators between God and his creation in Bible passages and their interpretation in such a way that one could reach a biblically based but also intellectual, rational, and honest exegesis. Neither of these two aspects should be omitted or put aside by his assertions because his aim was a synthesis that didn't abandon his strict monotheism and God's monarchy.[186] Arius presents an academic—that is, a scholarly theoretical—interpretation in contrast to an ecclesiastical interpretation that is strictly indebted to tradition, especially the *lex orandi*. The a priori focal point of his criteriology is the strict absoluteness of God. Everything else must be subordinated to God; one must therefore think of God as subsistent, uncreated, without beginning, and immutable. According to Arian theology, God's subsistence requires that no inner différance or differentiation can exist in God; otherwise, he wouldn't be the primary cause of all creation.[187]

According to Arius, one must think of the Son as being qualitatively on a lower level than God the Father because only God can be uncreated and every other (created) entity is dependent upon him. Nevertheless, God the Father gives precedence to the Son over the rest of creation because the Logos was created in truth and beyond time. Nevertheless, he has an originator: God who is uncreated, without beginning.[188] For him, the Son is a middle-transcendent being. One of the problems in Arius's interpretation lies in the fact that the relation between Father

186. See Rowan Williams, *Arius: Heresy and Tradition*, rev. ed. (Grand Rapids, MI: William B. Eerdmans, 2002), 111.
187. See Thomas Böhm, *Die Christologie des Arius: Dogmengeschichtliche Überlieferung unter besonderer Berücksichtigung der Hellenisierungsfrage* (St. Ottilien, Germany: EOS Verlag, 1991), 53.
188. See Williams, *Arius*, 96–97; and Böhm, *Christologie*, 53–54.

and Son isn't understood to be equiprimordial. God is the Father and is conditioned through neither origin nor change, whereas the Son is dependent on the Father for his existence and originated from the Father outside of time. Arius rejects the idea that there is any kind of ontological quality in their relation because this would imply the idea that God could change over time by becoming a father (Vatersein).[189] One can therefore assert that Arius's intellectual starting point is better situated in the field of philosophy than in the doctrine of the Trinity that is intrinsic to the history of salvation despite his repeated affirmations of his loyalty to church tradition.[190] Arius's deviation from church tradition isn't necessarily included in doctrine because it is in the process of being developed and is instead primarily focused on doxology and liturgy (lex orandi—lex credendi);[191] this becomes the main point of Athanasius of Alexandria's criticism:

> Arius is accused of teaching, on his own authority, an interpretation of Scripture at odds with the mind of the Church. It is not that there is an established "ecclesiastical" reading of the controversial passages that Arius deliberately spurns; Athanasius clearly has to work very hard to develop an alternative exegesis to that of his opponents. The point is, presumably, that Arius' interpretations are "private" in so far as they undermine the actual faith and practice of the Catholic Church: Alexander and Athanasius both appeal to the fact that Christ is worshipped as divine, Athanasius challenges the Arians to make sense of the baptismal rite on their theological presuppositions. Arius' readings are thus *de facto* divisive. *Lex orandi lex interpretandi* is Athanasius' governing rule; but Arius . . . evidently believes that, so long as the fundamental *regula fidei* is not disturbed, scriptural elucidation by duly qualified teachers may provide a critique of popular religious practice, or, at least, may oblige the initiate, the mature Christian, to reinterpret such practice when he or she is involved in it.[192]

189. See Böhm, *Christologie*, 54; and Williams, *Arius*, 96–98. God becomes the Father through the condition of the Son's (Jesus's) birth, even though God mustn't know change.
190. See Williams, *Arius*, 96.
191. Although this axiom was formulated at a later time, it was repeatedly used as the guiding principle for examining the orthodoxy of theological ideas. In the process, liturgy was considered a site of active faith that academic theology was to use as a standard. See Arno Schilson, "Lex orandi—lex credenda," in *LThK*, vol. 6, cols. 871–72.
192. Williams, *Arius*, 110.

According to Williams, Arius, through his own interpretation, situates himself outside the ecclesiastical community by relativizing lived ecclesiastical faith as an authoritative interpretive horizon and by presenting academic theology as a corrective.[193] Because God's grandeur and Absoluteness determine Arius's mindset so strongly, barely any space is given to the soteriological quality of Jesus Christ, and that is why Christ's redemptive event does not count for him as God's self-revelation.

The theological writings of the monk Eutyches are another attempt to illuminate Jesus Christ's work of salvation and his relevance for humanity. His answer should not be viewed as a philosophical speculation about the being of Jesus Christ, based on a higher striving for knowledge, that had gotten out of hand. He is interested in the classic example of "the favorite idea of popular Eastern piety,"[194] from which the conclusion is drawn not that God's solidarity with humanity stems from God's incarnation but rather that man himself, in an extension of Platonic anthropology, is deified through God's incarnation and ascends up to him.[195] Humanity's ascension toward God is central in Eutyches's conception of deification and overshadows the ignobility of Christ's kenosis into human flesh. As a consequence, this conception leads to an asymmetry in favor of the divinity:

> When Christ had accepted an earthly body and an animal soul, but not a human spirit; and when, to the contrary, the divine logos itself had replaced this, then the God-man was surely "of two natures" before becoming man, but not in "two natures" after the incarnation. In becoming man, the divine principle of life of the logos had deified the assumed flesh. And now Christ is our model for all things. So the deification of each individual person by necessity followed from established Platonic philosophy, and from the deification of human nature in Christ, provided that the individual was a member of the Body of Christ, and ate and drank of Christ's flesh and blood, and allowed the sacraments to have an effect on them—physically, spiritually, and intellectually.

193. See Williams, 87–91, 110.
194. Horst Dallmayr, *Die grossen vier Konzilien: Nicaea, Konstantinopel, Ephesus, Chalcedon* (Munich, Germany: Kösel, 1961), 206.
195. See Heinrich Bacht, "Die Rolle des orientalischen Mönchtums in den kirchenpolitischen Auseinandersetzungen um Chalkedon, 431–519," in *Das Konzil von Chalkedon: Geschichte und Gegenwart*, vol. 2, *Entscheidung um Chalkedon*, ed. Aloys Grillmeier and Heinrich Bacht (Würzburg, Germany: Echter Verlag, 1953), 311.

> It was the richness of these irreplaceable demands by these fervent, pious hearts that made Monophysitism the most attractive and successful heresy prior to Luther.[196]

This very human wish for salvation and acceptance at God's side thereby inclined so far to one extreme that when Eutyches attempted to resolve the mystery of Jesus Christ's human reality through Platonic anthropology, he reached theologically questionable conclusions due to the wishful thinking inherent in popular piety, and he also supported this theology in church policy for the benefit of Alexandrian monasticism.[197] He defended his own theology with great vehemence, without making concessions to the results of previous theological discussions.[198] Eutyches's side never developed a *sentire cum ecclesia* because he opposed the theological implications of the Formula of Union of 433, and instead of seeking consensus through a common striving for the truth, he irrevocably cemented his own position with vehement denials.[199] This led to a nonconsensual extreme position of (Alexandrian) unification Christology. Eutyches deviates from the continuous line of efforts to achieve consensus and attempts, via the so-called Robber Synod, not only to be reinstated but also to annul the consensual agreements of 433 in order to tilt the orthodoxy in the direction of Alexandrian theology and take it to the extreme of a strictly Monophysite theology.[200]

In response to the one-sidedness of the so-called Robber Synod, the Council of Chalcedon (under pressure from the emperor and his wife) reached a compromise

196. Dallmayr, *Konzilien*, 207.
197. See Bacht, "Rolle," 206–9.
198. One can therefore speculate that the earlier Council of Ephesus was only recognized and considered valid because a reconciliatory Formula of Unity was imposed after the council that avoided controversial ideas and thereby also theological standpoints and, all in all, reached a milder, more reconciliatory tone. Representatives didn't rigorously stick to the standpoint of their own theological school but rather acknowledged the concerns of the opposing party; this made it possible to reach a consensus that prepared the way for theological discussions at Chalcedon. See also Ernst Dassmann, *Kirchengeschichte 2/2: Theologie und innerkirchliches Leben bis zum Ausgang der Spätantike* (Stuttgart, Germany: Kohlhammer, 1999), 72, 87–89.
199. See Aloys Grillmeier, "Die theologische und sprachliche Vorbereitung der christologischen Formel von Chalkedon," in *Das Konzil von Chalkedon: Geschichte und Gegenwart*, vol. 1, *Der Glaube von Chalkedon*, ed. Aloys Grillmeier and Heinrich Bacht (Würzburg, Germany: Echter Verlag, 1951), 197. Eutyches's refusal to accept Christ's dual natures is expressed in the final sentence of his interrogation, which also led to his condemnation: "I profess that the Lord was made 'out of two natures' before the union, and I profess only 'one nature' after the union." In advance of the trial against Eutyches, Patricius Florentius clarified the horizon of thought of the Formula of Union: "Whoever does not say 'out of two natures' and 'two natures' isn't thinking correctly." Grillmeier, 197.
200. See Grillmeier, "Vorbereitung," 198.

between the Alexandrian and the Antiochian schools in which both could retain their theological positions but were not allowed to dismiss the other's position.[201] This, as it were, symmetrical balance between the positions of both schools made it possible for the Chalcedonian Symbolon to take on an intermediary role with an enormous power for integration that didn't claim to define the mystery of Christ's essence and illuminate it rationally. Only the core aspects of Jesus Christ's dual nature were defined based on theological tradition, whereas the inner personal mystery of the incarnation, founded on grace, did not fall victim to theological speculation.[202] The personal mystery of Jesus Christ consists in the fact that both his divine and his human natures exist in relationship to one another "without confusion or change, without division or separation" in such a way that "the character proper to each of the two natures was preserved as they came together in one Person and one hypostasis" (*DH*, 302).

The magnitude of the council's achievement can be seen in its creation of a framework, based on tradition, that validates Jesus Christ's dual nature and recognizes the theological intentions of both schools yet doesn't lapse into excessive speculation because this theological framework specifically leaves the personal mystery of Christ's being in two natures blank and doesn't attempt to define it.[203] The council fathers show thereby that God's divinity is not subordinated to human reason.

One can view both of these church councils as paradigms for the development of church doctrine. Council texts don't emerge in a vacuum of traditions and theories, unaware of différance in or challenges to previously determined matters. As a rule, they are based on disputes and conflicts between various or even opposing schools that aspire to put into words the mystery of faith that was revealed by Jesus Christ. It needs to be borne in mind that it is not only upon reflection but rather a basic principle that revelation and its testimony, and its development into doctrine, are

201. See Dassmann, *Kirchengeschichte*, 2/2:100.
202. See Ignacio Oritz de Urbina, "Das Glaubenssymbol von Chalkedon—sein Text, sein Werden, seine dogmatische Bedeutung," in Grillmeier and Bacht, *Das Konzil von Chalkedon*, 1:401–11.
203. See Urbina: "It is made clear here that the mysterious character of the incarnation isn't resolved through the conceptual language of the Church. To the contrary, the resolution is to be found in the two Christological heresies that were denounced in Ephesus and Chalcedon. One of the false doctrines doesn't want to accept the true unity of Being (*Seins-Einheit*) and personal unity between God and man; the other one wants to let man flow into God. True incarnation of a human depends on seeing God and man being connected, 'without confusion' and 'without division,' in one person" (1:410).

not at all identical.[204] A heresy per se should not only be viewed negatively; despite all its theological arrogance regarding the mystery of faith, a heresy entails an advance in knowledge: "Many things of importance to the Catholic faith are stirred up by the heat of the heretics' restlessness, and, because it is necessary to defend them against attack, they are therefore examined all the more diligently, understood all the more clearly, and proclaimed all the more imperatively. Thus, a question raised by an adversary becomes an opportunity for instruction."[205]

The problem of heresy doesn't principally stem from its location outside the church community—a prerequisite for taking up an opposing position. By trusting unduly in one's own orthodoxy, an interpretive perspective can misjudge its own particularity as if it were authoritative and correct in a way that one's own interpretative authority becomes so strongly tied to one's own perspective that one is unable to take note of the relativity of one's own view and recognize the validity of other perspectives.[206] This alone may lead to great difficulties in philosophic matters, but it becomes all the more precarious if one considers this from a theological point of view. Due to the one-sidedness of a theological school, one excludes oneself not only from an interpretive community of the church, but a heretic also shuts himself off from the hermeneutic introduction to the truth through the Holy Spirit—it is the Holy Spirit who fundamentally makes the event of faith, founded on grace, possible and also leads one to a deeper truth (John 14:17; 14:26; 16:13). The path then leads to heresy when (1) one places oneself outside the church community that is determined by Catholicism and owes its fundamental existence first

204. See Walter Kasper, "Tradition als theologisches Erkenntnisprinzip," in *Dogmengeschichte und katholische Theologie*, ed. Werner Löser, Karl Lehmann, and Matthias Lutz-Bachmann (Würzburg, Germany: Echter Verlag, 1985): "Christian faith believes in this one self-revelation and self-transmission in the Church and with the Church, and therefore, also in the transmitted linguistic and symbolic forms of the Church, but it doesn't actually believe in the Church and its doctrinal formulations. Because the ecclesiastical documents of tradition that have been handed down are of such importance, they must be preserved with reverence. However, one must guard against making them into Absolutes and thereby idols. As visible signs, they have the ability to transcend themselves into the unfathomable mystery of God. Finally, they have a doxological structure" (397). In this regard, doctrines are evidence of faith and hope.

205. Augustine, *The City of God against the Pagans*, ed. and trans. R. W. Dyson (Cambridge: Cambridge University Press, 1998), 695.

206. Arius, Eutyches, Joachim of Fiore, and many others were so convinced of their own orthodoxy that they were unable to recognize the conditionality of their own views and that their statements of interpretive authority placed them outside the interpretive community of the church. The reciprocal relationship between the subject and the community was terminated. See Eusebius, *The Church History of Eusebius*, in *Nicene and Post-Nicene Fathers*, 2nd ser., ed. Philip Schaff and Henry Wace, trans. C. A. Heurtley (Peabody, MA: Hendrickson, 1994), 1:248. See also Meuffels, *Gott*, 54.

and foremost to the revelation of the Holy Spirit and/or (2) one shuts oneself off from further instruction in questions of faith regarding the hermeneutic function of the Holy Spirit because one is now treating the explanation of God's divinity no longer as divine information but as a human response.[207]

Because the church's doctrinal statements do not represent purely human statements, and their authority is based on the fact that they are ecclesiastical statements and are therefore regarded as the result of the capacity for a human-divine synthesis (LG 8, 854), it is valid to also take into consideration revelation about God's essence. If Jesus Christ's message of salvation is summarized in the statement that God is love (1 John 4:8), then the relational structure of God, who retains his own personal dignity in the Holy Spirit—precisely as the God of love—can be understood as follows: love is the basis for this reciprocally revealing bond that recognizes the singularity of the Other and supports its existence so that one can achieve one's own independence in an enhanced way. Opposites are embedded in an expanded horizon that doesn't gloss over differences that would rob them of their singularity but rather prevents them from being isolated from one another or verging toward hostility toward one another. Augustine describes this loving community of God within himself in this way:[208]

> So when we say "the gift of the giver" and "the giver of the gift," we say each with reference to the other. So the Holy Spirit is a kind of inexpressible communion or fellowship of Father and Son, and perhaps he is given this name just because the same name can be applied to the Father and the Son. He is properly called what they are called in common, seeing that both Father and Son are holy and both Father and Son are spirit. So to signify the communion of them both by a name which applies to them both, the gift of both is called the Holy Spirit. And this three is one only God, good, great, eternal, omnipotent: his own unity, godhead, greatness, goodness, eternity, omnipotence.[209]

207. See Schmaus, *GdK*, vol. 1/1, 189–90.
208. Michael Schmaus, following Augustine, understands the dialectic of independence and simultaneous dialogical structure as the essential element of personhood; God is therefore the highest form of personality. Through his ability to imitate God, man himself can only find the fulfillment of his personhood (Perssonseins) in dialogue with God. See Schmaus, *GdK*, vol. 3, 166–70; see also Schmaus, vol. 2, 194–95.
209. Augustine, *The Works of Saint Augustine: A Translation for the 21st Century*, ed. John E. Rotelle, trans. Edmund Hill, vol. 1/5, *The Trinity / De Trinitate* (Hyde Park, NY: New City Press, 2015), 242–43.

This explanation is of relevance to ecclesiastical statements because the church, due to its pneumatological foundation, is the sacramental space for communicating God's love in the world; this space is the Holy Spirit himself within the Trinitarian event. Thus man's faith isn't only made possible through the Holy Spirit, but in addition, through his community-building effect on the faith of the church, man's faith relies on the church.[210] The person of the Holy Spirit is therefore considered the structural guarantor of the ecclesiastical community and faith.[211]

If one applies the previous analysis to the church and the unfolding of its doctrinal history, one can argue the following: when theological schools emerge and take seriously the (theologically honest) concerns of differing schools with love, respect, and recognition—and without going against their own principles, concerns, and theological points of view in a way that would lead to a loss of identity—then the various concerns can attain a higher synthesis through joint attempts to gain knowledge. God's will for salvation finds its highest expression in love because all law also finds its fulfillment in love. Through the act of love, God's will for salvation at the end of time is brought to fruition in man and to proleptic completion (Gal 5:14; Matt 22:39; Rom 13:8–10; John 13:34–35; 1 John 3:23–24).[212]

A proposed council document can only be determined to have attained and to continue to hold true authority in the church after the time period of the council; in this way, it also attains its authority through tradition. The church has always been guided and led by the Holy Spirit and can therefore recognize, accept, and also indirectly acknowledge, through faith effected by the Spirit, that the documents of the church that have been handed down are indeed authentic, authoritative, and thus (in large part) testimonials informed by the Holy Spirit.[213] In order to consider the question of

210. See Kehl, *Kirche*, 68–75.

211. See Walter Kasper, *The Catholic Church: Nature, Reality and Mission*, ed. R. David Nelson, trans. Thomas Hoebel (London: Bloomsbury, 2015): "Yet, as Christ continues to live in the Holy Spirit in the Church, the Church can never stop being the Church of Jesus Christ. . . . The Church as a whole cannot fall into error, that is, it cannot lapse from the Gospel and proclaim a different gospel" (166). See also Augustine, *The Works of Saint Augustine: A Translation for the 21st Century*, ed. Allan D. Fitzgerald, trans. Edmund Hill, vol. 1/12, *Homilies on the Gospel of John 1–40* (Hyde Park, NY: New City Press, 2009): "We too, then, receive the Holy Spirit, if we love the Church, if we are united by charity, if we rejoice in the Catholic name and faith. Let us believe, brothers and sisters, that to the extent that someone loves the Church of Christ, to that extent he has the Holy Spirit" (521).

212. See Wilhelm Egger, *Galater Brief, Philipperbrief, Philemonbrief* (Würzburg, Germany: Echter Verlag, 1988): "The law is fulfilled, i.e., brought to perfection . . . because God's will is expressed in its purest form in his commandment to love, and the deepest meaning of all commandments is found in this commandment" (37).

213. See Kasper, *Church*, 135–36.

tradition more broadly and ask about the criteria of Catholic faith in regard to content, I shall follow Vincent of Lérins's criteria for Catholic faith: "Moreover, in the Catholic Church itself, all possible care must be taken, that we hold that faith which has been believed everywhere, always, by all. For that is truly and in the strictest sense 'Catholic,' which, as the name itself and the reason of the thing declare, comprehends all universally. This rule we shall observe if we follow universality, antiquity, consent."[214]

Even if Vincent of Lérins only uses past tense verb forms here ("which has been believed"), the characteristic style of his observations shows that it is not a matter of a past event when it comes to matters of faith because the past (with its traditions) is one of the factors that establishes its present-day accuracy and validity. Instead of understanding Catholicism as a concept of a confessional containment, one does it more justice if one views it as one of the four *notae ecclesiae* (one, holy, catholic, and apostolic)[215] and emphasizes universality as a characteristic of Catholicism.[216] This includes a geographic and a temporal universality; it allows the faith of the church to recognize a synchronous as well as diachronic structure.[217]

Tradition and Catholicism can be harmoniously blended in such a way that tradition makes visible the eternal community of the faithful. Tradition isn't a fossilized artifact whose value only lies in passing down very old things; rather, tradition has direction and is future oriented. Something is passed down because it will be relevant and of value in the future—tradition only becomes sustainable and forward looking when the respective subject grasps it not from a neutral perspective but rather with an attitude of anticipation and implementation.[218] One must understand its relevance to one's own life; otherwise, tradition degenerates and becomes part of the decor.

For faith to be of relevance to one's own life, and thereby have an existential dimension, it doesn't only depend on the particular person. Faith is a synthesis of divine and human elements. The initiative and the call to faith originate from God; for this

214. Vincent, *Commonitory*, 11:132 (2, 5–6).
215. See Kehl, *Kirche*, 68, 95, 125–31.
216. Kehl's work makes it possible to harmonize the sanctity of the church with this idea of universality because the church is the community of the faithful. See Kehl, *Kirche*: "Not only the living, but also everyone who has been blessed by Christ in the past, present, and future, belongs to this community of the faithful. The Church embraces those who have been completed by faith, i.e., all those who participate in a definitive and incontestable way in the life of the resurrected Christ. Pilgrims and the completed Church together build the community of the Body of Christ" (128).
217. See Kasper, *Church*, 176.
218. See Kasper, "Tradition," 382, 392.

synthesis to succeed, this call must be followed by acceptance and a response on the human side.[219] God's incomprehensibility also includes the incomprehensibility of the third hypostasis: the Holy Spirit is neither accessible nor comprehensible to man. This implies, especially in regard to the history of doctrine, that it is impossible for faith to be manipulated through the Holy Spirit. It is therefore up to humans to give space to and be receptive to the Holy Spirit so that the Holy Spirit can act without being undermined by man's claims to biased interpretations in his hermeneutic function.

It would therefore be an ideal situation in the progress of doctrinal history if a theological school of thought didn't only insist on its own interpretive authority but instead expressed its request and concern in a communal struggle to find proper language to express the truth. Another school of thought will likewise be granted space to present its concern so that through joint recognition of their respective theological positions, they can create a *common space* for the Holy Spirit of love, who will lead to the truth (John 16:13): this would provide authoritative proof of the church as a synthesis of the divine and the human. The *fides qua* and *fides quae*, in accordance with the binary division of faith, can be classified as follows: The *fides qua* can be described as the possibility of faith, as revealed by God, that man answers in the affirmative. The *fides quae* builds on this; it attempts to understand the guaranteed and accepted possibility of faith and the ongoing attempt to articulate it in language. This attempt is granted legitimacy, validity, and authority as a *depositum fidei* only if it doesn't alienate due to human interpretive arrogance and is subsequently recognized by the faith of the church, as guided by the Holy Spirit.

The Holy Spirit is the hermeneutic interpreter of divine truth and thereby preserves the church with its faith "uncorrupt and inviolate, in the sanctity of a perpetual virginity and truth";[220] this also demonstrates the protective function of the Holy Spirit for the church. The Holy Spirit guides the church throughout the ages and prevents any heretical aberration from becoming a permanent guarantor of the truth. To be sure, heresies arise and may also take up space in the ecclesiastical horizon of thought, as the long battle against Arianism makes abundantly clear, but they don't become part of the *depositum fidei* of the church in the long run. In retrospect, one can recognize a universal willingness to engage in the intellectual endeavor—but it

219. See Schmaus, *GdK*, vol. 1/1, 5.
220. Novatian, *Treatise concerning the Trinity*, in *Ante-Nicene Fathers*, ed. Alexander Roberts and James Donaldson, trans. Robert Ernest Wallis (Peabody, MA: Hendrickson, 1994), 5:641.

wasn't de facto there.[221] The Holy Spirit guarantees the unity of the church and faith because he is the *one* Spirit who ensures *one* faith within *one* church. Straying from this one faith implies that a heretic is also simultaneously excluding himself from this one church because he lacks the faith to trust the unifying function of the Spirit.

It is not of primary importance to focus on the collapse of a consensus of faith in the unifying power of the Holy Spirit. The enduring, timeless consensus of church tradition—it has lasted some twenty-one centuries—is far more significant in considering the being of the church. Wherever one can find a consensus within the church—defined and granted through the work of the Holy Spirit—one can interpret the Holy Spirit as a sign that refers to the authority and validity of church doctrine.[222] The close connection between tradition and consensus within the internal structure of the church can be confirmed by the common profession of faith. The uninterrupted continuum of the *regula fidei*, going all the way back to its apostolic origin as an authentic tradition of the church, was decisive for Tertullian, who defended the unbroken transmission of the *one* faith that was founded and established by Jesus Christ himself.[223]

To recognize this timeless and supraregional consensus, sharing the same faith is more necessary than a straightforward statement entailing the same vocabulary. With the development of the *regula fidei*—that is, the profession of faith—another tool was developed for determining if one was, and still is, in agreement with this consensus and therefore a member of the ecclesiastical community or whether, by rejecting it, one has placed oneself outside the church.[224] A valid consensus

221. The minimal response can be traced back to man attributing an excessive role to his own interpretive authority—that is, man's assertion that he is the only one with correct answers. This means that man grants too small a role to the divine due to his lack of love for and trust in the Holy Spirit's message of truth. If one wants to present this as a binary juxtaposition, then man's claim to interpretive power presents itself as a discourse between authorities. Hope and trust revoke this discourse based on power.
222. A sign refers to something else and, therefore, isn't the signified itself; only a formal consensus of a signifier does not imply per se the automatic pneumatological legitimacy of its content as a signified.
223. See Tertullian, *The Prescription against Heretics*, in *Ante-Nicene Fathers*, ed. Alexander Roberts and James Donaldson, trans. Peter Holmes (Peabody, MA: Hendrickson, 1994), 3:252. See also Thomas Böhm, "Glaube und Inkulturation: Gab es einen 'Zwang' zur Heterodoxie in der Spätantike?," in *Glaube und Kultur: Begegnung zweier Welten?*, ed. Thomas Böhm in collaboration with Benedikt Barth (Freiburg, Germany: Herder, 2009), 115.
224. The assertion that the drawing up of creeds in formulaic language of faith was done in an inappropriate, fixed form and thus led to ossification is untenable. One can draw a direct line from the New Testament testimonials to the doctrines of church history because Jesus Christ's kerygma in the New Testament was not intended to be unreflective and purely enthusiastic speech but already contained formulaic summaries of faith: the praesymbola. See Söll, *Das Dasein im Glauben*, 1/5:25–26.

that transcends one's current time and place can't be recognized immediately. The binary structure of signs (signifier and signified) of the profession of faith is a frame of reference and a tool for making distinctions: the Symbolon of the church. According to Rufinus, this resulted in constant hostility from outside the church and heretical aberrations from within:

> Being on the eve therefore of departing from one another, they first mutually agreed upon a standard of their future preaching, lest haply, when separated, they might in any instance vary in the statements which they should make to those whom they should invite to believe in Christ. Being all therefore met together, and being filled with the Holy Ghost, they composed, as we have said, this brief formulary of their future preaching, each contributing his several sentence to one common summary: and they ordained that the rule thus framed should be given to those who believe.
>
> To this formulary, for many and most sufficient reasons, they gave the name or Symbol. For Symbol . . . in Greek answers to both "Indicium" (a sign or token) and "Collatio" (a joint contribution made by several) in Latin. . . . The Apostles therefore prescribed this formulary as a sign or token by which he who preached Christ truly, according to Apostolic rule, might be recognized.[225]

Even though God himself gives the church, on its pilgrimage through time, necessary assurances regarding their destination (LG 1–6, 849–51), Cardinal Bellarmine's designation of the church as *societas perfecta* partially obscures its historical dimension because perfection is a condition of stasis and thereby completion.[226] Instead of focusing on perfection, one should focus more on divinely conditioned perfectibility and teleological directedness because "here on earth the church is on pilgrimage from the Lord (see 2 Cor 5; 6), it is like an exile" (LG 6, 852). In this

225. Rufinus, *A Commentary on the Apostles' Creed*, in *Nicene and Post-Nicene Fathers*, 2nd ser., ed. Philip Schaff and Henry Wace, trans. William Henry Fremantle (Peabody, MA: Hendrickson, 1994), 3:542. Even though Rufinus portrays the apostolic past idealistically, his presentation is nevertheless of value for this investigation because it shows unequivocally that it's been necessary to guarantee, in terms of content, an equanimity in faith ever since the apostolic beginnings.
226. See Joseph Ratzinger, *Das Problem der Dogmengeschichte in der Sicht der katholischen Theologie* (Cologne: Westdeutscher Verlag, 1966): "One may only speak of history where real progress and personal development take place; simply identifying everything that remains the same doesn't create history" (9).

process of a historical pilgrimage toward the kingdom of the Father, the church is also aware of its own need for process (LG 5, 851). The church isn't a monolith; to the contrary, it possesses an essential inner plurality (1 Cor 12:12–14; LG 9, 855) because the structure and message of the church are universal, for all peoples (Matt 28:19). The purpose of the church is clear and guaranteed on the divine side; in contrast, the path of the church is precarious because being human involves, at the very least, detours and wrong turns. For the church in structural terms, a coordinating network is necessary for corrections so that the wandering people don't lose their way or even go astray amid the thicket of theological-philosophical interpretations and perspectives because the Holy Spirit, due to his divine mode of action, is unavailable to man. This corrective and coordinating system can be recognized in the tradition that protects the *depositum fidei* from unauthorized distortions, alienations, and false innovations, especially those that appeared at the time of the Church Fathers. This explains why a heretic, due to his opposition to or straying away from the *depositum fidei*, was understood at that time as a person who lacks tradition.[227]

However, one mustn't view tradition as a fixed mindset that transforms the living message of Christ at a later time into a lifeless corpus of writings. A proper understanding of tradition requires an acknowledgment that traditions are worth handing down. Anyone who views a profession of faith without a living and heartfelt faith overlooks the fact that it is a statement of existential relevance; because a profession of faith becomes known through faith, it has a performative quality.[228] To illuminate aspects of tradition and the content of doctrine, in this context, tradition and doctrine are interpreted as an unfolding of a shared ecclesiastical faith and not in relationship to historical isolation.[229] Doctrines of the church are

227. See Söll, *Das Dasein im Glauben*, 1/5:71. It is therefore easy to view all of patristics, in its adherence to apostolic faith, as a nonstop fight against heresy.

228. See Kasper, *Dogma*: "This understanding is still very much alive today because, in accordance with academic theology, the objective tradition (id, quo traditur) and the active tradition (actus, quo traditur) together build an indivisible whole, so that one can never have faith outside of, and beyond one's current testimony of faith. This means that faith isn't only a belief that individual doctrines are true; faith is a union of bearing witness and being witnessed, of faith and love. Faith, therefore, is the reality that has been witnessed and lived in the church, that can't be captured objectively in individual statements" (39). See also Karl Rahner, "What Is a Dogmatic Statement?," in *Theological Investigations*, vol. 5, *Later Writings*, trans. Karl-H. Kruger (Baltimore: Helicon, 1966), 48. Rahner speaks here in favor of overcoming an objective, statement-like understanding of a doctrinal statement. One should view it, instead, as integrated into the context of faith: *fides quae* and *fides qua* overlap when a doctrinal statement is a profession of faith.

229. See Kasper, *Dogma*, 27.

statements that lead into the *mysterium* of Christ; they are therefore not identical to it because the limits of language are constantly being transgressed by their overarching greatness and transcendence.[230] Doctrines are professions of faith; they are, first and foremost, statements of a hopeful faith. They have the structure of proofs that refer to a future completion that has already begun proleptically; this explains why doctrinal statements themselves can be both true and correct without losing their human conditionality.[231] Thus doctrine and tradition have an implicit element of openness and surplus rather than closedness because *Deus semper maior.*

Yet the form of a decision (e.g., the doctrinal statement of an ecumenical council) doesn't offer any guarantees that the council's decisions will be recognized and passed on. The Council of Serdica in 343 counts as a paradigm: at the highest level of doctrinal teaching—and at the instigation of the emperor in the West along with the approval of the emperor in the East—an attempt was made to once again bring together the theology of the East and the West that had been drifting apart. This attempt failed because the council broke into an Eastern and a Western synod at the very beginning, and the respective parties each denounced and excommunicated the leading bishops of the opposition.[232] Although the church's highest form of doctrinal teaching was used, the resolutions of the opposition were not recognized and therefore not passed on: the council had no effect on church doctrine.[233]

Joseph Ratzinger makes this point very clearly when he maintains that the Council of Serdica's ineffectiveness was due to its failed reception: "If something isn't recognized, it won't be effective; it remains ineffective and thereby unreal. Appropriation,

230. See Rahner, "Dogmatic Statement," 5:58. See Anselm, *Proslogion*: "id quo maius cogitari non potest" (116).

231. See Kasper, *Dogma*, 55, 104–5, 125.

232. See Adolf Martin Ritter, "Dogma und Lehre in der Alten Kirche," in *Handbuch der Dogmen- und Theologiegeschichte*, vol. 1, *Die Lehrentwicklung im Rahmen der Katholizität*, ed. Carl Andresen (Göttingen, Germany: Vandenhoeck & Ruprecht, 1982), 174–76. See also Dassmann, *Kirchengeschichte*, 2/2:44–45.

233. Even though the Council of Serdica was sporadically cited as an ecumenical council during the late seventh and early eighth centuries, and therefore appeared to be viewed as having doctrinal significance, the future reception of these early church councils was guided by Gregory the Great. The important councils of the early church are Nicaea, Constantinople, Ephesus, and Chalcedon; in this context, Gregory considered these four councils to be analogous to the four evangelists of the New Testament. See also Klaus Schatz, "Rezeption ökumenischer Konzilien im ersten Jahrtausend: Schwierigkeiten, Formen der Bewältigung und verweigerte Rezeption," in *Glaube als Zustimmung: Zur Interpretation kirchlicher Rezeptionsvorgänge*, ed. Wolfgang Beinert (Freiburg, Germany: Herder, 1991), 106.

assimilation, and transformation only happen through recognition."[234] The fact that the entire church (i.e., the entire bishopry) is not represented at an ecumenical council yet asserts that it is able to speak for the entire ecclesiastical οἰκουμένη, must be understood as a leap of faith and an anticipatory acceptance in regard to the *sensus fidelium* (LG 12, 858).[235] The faithful of the church aren't in a merely passive position through the sealing function of their reception in *sensus fidelium*; rather, through their reception, they are active participants in a dialogical event in the emergence of doctrine.[236]

The attitude of the magisterium toward the church can also be viewed as analogous to the attitude of the ordained priesthood to the common priesthood of the faithful. It is an internal counterpart that can't exist without the other because it is directed toward its counterpart.[237] The subordination or superordination of one part to the other is the result of a misunderstanding because they are structurally on the same level. The magisterium is to be understood as a counterpart within the church; it is responsible for protecting the *depositum fidei* from subjective access and from an overly subjective application of interpretive authority.[238] The magisterium therefore provides a structure for correction, but it can only carry out its responsibilities with integrity if it knows that it belongs to the entirety of the church and has a serving function for the rest of the church.[239] The *sensus fidelium* is not a *sensus hierarchicus*: the entire laity, by definition, can't be led into error because it is guided by the Holy Spirit.[240]

234. Joseph Ratzinger, *Das neue Volk Gottes: Entwürfe zur Ekklesiologie* (Düsseldorf, Germany: Patmos Verlag, 1970), 150, cited in Johanna Rahner, "Lehramt und Glaubenssinn: Anmerkungen zu einem zunehmend schwieriger werdenden dogmatischen Lehrstück," in Knapp and Söding, *Glaube in Gemeinschaft*, 176. See also Ratzinger, *Problem*, 39.
235. See Schatz. "Rezeption," 95.
236. See J. Rahner, "Lehramt," 174–77. The fact that Mary is free of original sin is evidence that the *sensus fidelium* becomes problematic as soon as it is no longer viewed as bearing witness to one's faith and instead functions as a justification of faith. Here, the *sensus fidelium* has a generative function. See Gisbert Greshake, *Maria-Ecclesia: Perspektiven einer marianisch grundierten Theologie und Kirchenpraxis* (Regensburg, Germany: F. Pustet, 2014), 254–55, 289.
237. See Kehl, *Kirche*, 432–33, 116.
238. Arius and Eutyches are the prime examples; their subjective interpretations were doctrinally restricted and condemned.
239. See J. Rahner, "Lehramt," 179. See Hermann Josef Pottmeyer, "Rezeption und Gehorsam—Aktuelle Aspekte einer wiederentdeckten Realität 'Rezeption,'" in Beinert, *Glaube als Zustimmung*, 78–80.
240. See Werbick, "Autorität": "This would require humility in the face of authority from all sides" (30). See also Werbick, 35. This is even valid for the church without the Ministry of Doctrine because it would be a radical misunderstanding if the contemporary church viewed itself as the ultimate manifestation of the will of the Holy Spirit. The universality of the church spans generations and therefore encompasses both the past and the future.

> On a human level, therefore, the entire Church with all its members is primarily responsible for the formation of doctrine and the promised infallibility of the Church; individual members only secondarily receive special ministerial services that serve the construction of the whole (Rom 12:4ff; 1 Cor 12:4ff) and the *confirmatio fratrum*. . . .
>
> One can define a doctrine, in passing, as the place where the Church becomes definitively conscious of its own faith and thereby recognizes its faith as permanent and binding. The Church's self-awareness, however, doesn't happen through a monologue with itself; rather, it always occurs in dialogue with its historically prescribed revelation. . . . The Church doesn't pocket the Word of God and make it into a possession; The Word of God remains above the Church and is in each case prescribed for it.[241]

Because the *sensus fidelium* isn't easily accessible to the laity and is an event of grace through the work of the Holy Spirit, Walter Kasper proposes the following criteria in order to show the validity of individual traditions as parts within the one, larger, whole tradition.[242] First of all, Kasper makes it clear that this merciful Holy Spirit is the Spirit of Jesus Christ and that no profession of faith is possible other than to Jesus Christ (1 Cor 12:3: "Therefore I want you to understand that no one speaking by the Spirit of God ever says 'Let Jesus be cursed!' and no one can say 'Jesus is Lord' except by the Holy Spirit"). Therefore, all traditions must demonstrate their relation to the redemptive event of the incarnation, the cross, and the resurrection. Kasper's second criterion shows that the Holy Spirit urges the faithful to read Scripture in a spiritual sense and not to get stuck on a literal reading of the surface of the text.[243] It is the Holy Spirit, in his divinity, who gives life (John 6:63); Scripture comes alive through spiritual guidance and thereby becomes the word of God.[244] In his third criterion, Kasper maintains that the Holy Spirit is not an isolating force but rather a force that brings together and unifies: the one Holy Spirit with his many and diverse gifts is this same unifying Spirit.

241. Kasper, *Dogma*, 27.
242. See Kasper, "Tradition," 400–402.
243. Based on this investigation, one can note that the spiritual *intentio operis* has a quality of surplus that exceeds the *intentio auctoris*.
244. See Kasper, "Tradition": "In essence, tradition is what the Church Fathers called the spiritual meaning of Scripture" (401). Through the assistance of the Holy Spirit, Scripture becomes an icon of God in which one can sense the transcendent greatness of God. See Marion, *God*, 18–20.

Through the work of the Holy Spirit, the church can be viewed as a well-tuned orchestra wherein the whole is greater than the sum of its parts—as the pneumatological and christological surplus of the visible church as the body of Christ (LG 8, 854). Thus it is the responsibility of pneumatological guidance to ensure that the consensus of the community isn't limited by the boundaries of a contemporary time period but rather includes the community of the faithful of all time in this all-encompassing event; the *sensus fidelium* is valid for the entirety of the church.[245] The magisterium exercises its sealing function when it officially confirms that a specific content is the faith of the church; this occurs in the format of an infallible profession of faith. The reason for this doesn't lie in a request from the ecclesiastical magisterium but rather is from the need to be able to confront both internal and external difficulties.[246]

Doctrinally approved professions of faith have a twofold purpose. Internally, they have a sealing function; faith has attained a certainty, a clarity in knowledge, that is worth preserving. The consensus that has been reached is put into a secure form that prevents new quarrels and uncertainty[247] without overcoming the fragility of faith in the process (2 Cor 4:7: "But we have this treasure in clay jars, so that it may be made clear that this extraordinary power belongs to God and does not come from us").

From the beginning of Christianity, it has been proclaimed that one mustn't falsify that which has been revealed. Instead, one must preserve with fidelity that which has been received (1 Cor 15:1–11; Gal 1:9). In contrast, to those outside the church, ecclesiastical statements are testimonials of the truth that believers fulfill (1 Pet 3:15). But this isn't a relative or negotiable testimonial because the church is commenting here in an existential format. The church itself doesn't have sovereign power over language; therefore, even the church's (sworn) statements can become perjury.

This isn't evidence of a lack or deficiency; it confers on the church the possibility of using an existential format in its statements that alone, through the form of

245. Even if Cano's *De Locis* doctrine helped decisively in differentiating the topology of faith, the sense of faith isn't treated as a *locus theologicus* and therefore isn't acknowledged as an authority. See Mannes Dominikus Koster, "Von der Findung der theologischen Grundsätze," in *Einsicht und Glaube*, ed. Joseph Ratzinger and Heinrich Fries (Freiburg, Germany: Herder, 1962), 287.
246. See Söll, *Das Dasein im Glauben*, 1/5:47.
247. See Söll, 1/5:52–53, 60. The constant, painful experience of heresy tormented the church and forced it into the role of an apologist. The dilemma between progress and preservation therefore always tilted toward preservation.

these proclamations, emphasizes their importance and the strength of the church's convictions. The church appears here as a community of witnesses wherein the statements of the church depend on the ecclesiastical "I," though the emphasis of the statement is on the content for which one puts oneself at risk.[248] According to Hansjürgen Verweyen, "There is only one 'site' in the immensity of historical contingency where one can discern that something unconditional has truly become reality: a testimony, in which the witness views his own life as totally irrelevant in the face of what unconditionally makes demands of him."[249]

The statement doesn't become truer through its format and is therefore also no less affected by the fallibility of speech in general, but the statement becomes more trustworthy because the speaker puts himself at stake in his (sworn) statement—that is, the oath. The speaker puts himself at risk with his statement because he can't guarantee the content, since the form of the statement is inextricably tied to his own personhood. Therefore, one hopes for the trust (*fides*) of one's counterpart.[250]

The church can internally be understood as a place where the faithful have their own space to bear witness through the profession of faith that has been doctrinally sealed and handed down by the entirety of the faithful. Externally, the church is considered a collective subject that presents, in its (infallible) statements, radical evidence of its message of hope. The church's function to serve the world is granted existential weight through this message that also forms its identity. As a result, the church has a precarious identity that it can neither confer upon itself nor access on its own but is always part of an interconnected structure.[251]

One mustn't lose sight of the sacramental structure of the church because this significantly influences the perspective within the church. The church views itself, so to speak, as both a sign and an instrument, within temporality, for the union

248. See Agamben, *Sacrament*, 69. The oath is located at the dialectical intersection between a blessing and a curse because every oath can become a curse; in the process, the "I" becomes a perjurer and the *fides* is lost. The oath can also endure; in the process, the swearing "I" is increasingly respected as a witness. See also Agamben, 69–71.
249. Hansjürgen Verweyen, *Botschaft eines Toten? Den Glauben Rational Verantworten* (Regensburg, Germany: F. Pustet, 1997), 131.
250. See Agamben, *Sacrament*, 26–27. Thus the oath is a performative proof of the *fides* demand; one hopes to maintain trust through an oath. Likewise, "the proper context of the oath is therefore among those institutions, like the *fides*, whose function is to performatively affirm the truth and trustworthiness of speech. . . . The monotheistic religions, above all Christianity, inherit from the oath the centrality of faith in the word as the essential content of religious experience." Agamben, 65–66.
251. See Gregor Maria Hoff, *Ekklesiologie* (Paderborn, Germany: Ferdinand Schöningh, 2011), 11–13.

of God and the world in Christ (LG 1, 849).[252] Infallible statements of the church should therefore be viewed as infallible statements of hope[253] that have a proleptic role in God's infallibility because God works through his Holy Spirit.[254] They are and remain Christian theological statements that condition their self-conception, whereas the church itself prioritizes God's greatness above its own statements because the Absolute can't be comprehended in contingent statements—the ontological difference must be taken into account: "For between Creator and creature no similitude can be expressed without implying a greater dissimilitude" (*DH*, 806).[255]

For the remainder of this investigation, I use the following formal criteria to determine the validity of doctrine: (1) its content is a revealed truth; (2) it is presented in the form of a proposition;[256] (3) in its objective validity, it is an infallible statement of faith; (4) the individual believer is obligated to follow it; and (5) the statement (i.e., its textualization) happens through the church within its own historicity.[257] Therefore, one mustn't demand too much of doctrine by considering it to be the totality of Christianity and making it into a statement of identity between God and doctrine.

> Christian doctrine isn't the totality of Christianity and doesn't claim to simultaneously be the Christian way of life. The Church and theology have continuously, and rightly so, fought against having religious feeling, the so-called value of life, or the irresistible appeal to the *sensus fidelium* determine the concept and content of doctrine, and they have fought against broadening both, in the end, further than a doctrine-friendly theology of eschatology could. . . . The concept of "doctrine" doesn't exclude the possibility that its content is more than a teaching, and that it should above

252. See Hoff, *Ekklesiologie*, 12.
253. See Kasper, *Dogma*, 104, 125. Likewise, "there is no justification for theology to solve its difficulties on its own through an act of violence. This also applies to the relationship between doctrine and Scripture; faith must always be connected to hope." Kasper, 125.
254. See Agamben, *Sacrament*: "Language is the word of God, and the word of God is, in the words of Philo, an oath; it is God insofar as he reveals himself in the *logos* as the 'faithful one' (*pistos*) par excellence. God is the oath-taker in the language of which man is only the speaker, but in the oath on the name of God the language of men communicates with divine language" (49–50).
255. See Rahner, "Dogmatic Statement," 5:47, 50. God's superabundance can never be captured by a finite sign.
256. This makes it clear that *a* doctrine is a revealed truth, based on its content, but it isn't the revelation itself. Doctrine and revelation are *not identical*.
257. See Söll, *Das Dasein im Glauben*, 1/5:20.

> all produce more than knowledge; rather, its origin and history indicate sufficiently that it must, above all, be the truth and announce the truth.[258]

The form of doctrinal teaching is historically conditioned; it has developed through long struggles within the church.[259] Paradoxically, the Symbolon of Nicaea was one of the greatest obstacles to the development of the history of doctrine because nothing was allowed to be formulated after Nicaea until the Symbolon of Chalcedon. All synods and councils that took place between Nicaea and Chalcedon lacked authority to formulate their own doctrines or new ones. They were supposed to be pure exegesis of the Nicene Creed; they therefore examined their own orthodoxy on the basis of the Symbolon of Nicaea.[260]

Doctrine is the attempt to bridge the gap and to overcome the distance that lies between man's understanding of history and God's direct intervention in the human world through Jesus Christ's self-revelation and message, expressed in speech, of the coming of the kingdom of God at the end of time.[261] This is the existential statement of the pilgrim church.[262]

With Jesus Christ, revelation entered man's everyday world (DV 4, 972) in its fullness and in a definitive way; this led to man's attempts, during this span of time, to transform the relevance of this revelation into language. The truth of Jesus Christ is not abstract; it is addressed directly to humans, as recipients, so that they will attempt to make the greatness, significance, and relevance of Jesus Christ understandable through speech. This occurs as a synthesis that combines

258. Söll, 1/5:45.
259. See Söll, 1/5:10–11, 53. The first critical period in the definition of doctrine can be seen in Vincent of Lérins, who understood doctrine in the context of the truth of divine revelation that is passed on in the format of a *depositum fidei*. Vincent of Lérins's criticism of several passages in Augustine may have led to a very restrained reception of his own work and to the fact that a more conclusive examination of the definition of doctrine had to take a detour through the Counter-Reformation and then the First Vatican Council.
260. See Schatz, "Rezeption," 100–101.
261. See Söll, *Das Dasein im Glauben*, 1/5:52. According to Lacan, this is the attempt to transform the Real into the Symbolic. The fact that doctrine is an example of this attempt doesn't take anything away from its existentialist dimension. Even though man is unable to dominate God through language, he nevertheless puts himself at risk in his statements.
262. This is the reason Michael Schmaus seeks assurance that even the statements of the magisterium have been placed under the conditions of apophatic theology—in the long run, even the magisterium can't bridge the gap between the creator and the created (Schmaus, *GdK*, vol. 1/1, 82; likewise, *GdK*, vol. 1/2, 21). This is an attempt to bridge the gap between God and man through language; therefore, the matter of putting doctrine into language can be designated as a pastoral duty because of its supposed assistance to humans.

both the divine and the human.[263] Therefore, revelation and doctrine are not in a relationship of identity to one another; one does greater justice to doctrine if one views it as an *obligatory* movement by the church that leads to a deeper and more adequate understanding.[264]

Therefore, the historicity of revelation is what makes it possible for doctrine to advance human understanding. Historicity is not *primarily* a threat to doctrine; it makes doctrine possible.[265]

As beneficial as all of this sounds, it once again raises the following question: What can humans say about God? And the much more important question: How and why does that which has been said become valid? To be sure, man can say a lot about God. Martin Buber writes the following about the word *God*: "It is the most heavy-laden of all human words. None has become so soiled, so mutilated. . . . Generations of men have laid the burden of their anxious lives upon this word and weighed it to the ground; it lies in the dust and bears their whole burden. The races of man with their religious factions have torn the word to pieces; they have killed for it and died for it, and it bears their finger-marks and their blood."[266]

Man is free to use and also misuse the word *God*. God sent himself as Son and Logos into the world out of love; this was taken so far that Jesus Christ delivered himself to man for the sake of salvation (John 3:16). But God didn't deliver himself to man only as man; as the Word, God also offered himself to man by revealing his name in a dialectical manner. His Word is handed over to man in a dialectical but not an absolute manner. To be sure, man has dialectical access to the Word, but this does not imply sovereign power with simultaneous authority. Buber makes the point so forcefully when he writes that man can defile the Word—but this is only temporary defilement. Man does not have authority over the truth and the correct usage of God's name; proof of the validity of using God's name in human statements is far more dependent on God himself. It is therefore fitting to consider the use of God's name in the horizon of the historical development of doctrine.

The form of doctrinal specification does not per se guarantee that it will result in the anticipated effect. This is even more remarkable when a nonecclesiastical

263. See Söll, *Das Dasein im Glauben*, 1/5:52–53. See also Schmaus, *GdK*, vol. 1/1, 5.
264. See Söll, *Das Dasein im Glauben*, 1/5:19, 61.
265. See Söll, 1/5:53.
266. Martin Hoff, "Autobiographical Fragments," in *The Philosophy of Martin Buber*, ed. Paul Arthus Schilp and Maurice Friedman (La Salle, IL: Open Court, 1967), 30.

factor has a decisive influence. In late antiquity, an ecumenical council didn't attain its status just by the presence of bishops from the entire ecclesiastical community; the fact that it was convened by the emperor, who invited the bishops of the ecclesiastical community to gather and pass resolutions, was the decisive, formal criterion.[267]

In this context, the Council of Serdica was proclaimed by both the Eastern and the Western emperors for the purpose of settling a doctrinal dispute concerning Arianism and its hypostatic terminology.[268] The political goal—to restore unity to the empire—failed from the start because the council immediately broke into separate West and East synods. Both the Western and the Eastern sides drafted and adopted doctrinal texts in which they reciprocally excommunicated the leading bishops and never clarified the theological problem.[269] Even if, in the short run, the Council of Serdica was considered a proper synod—that is, a properly seated and representative council[270]—in the long run, its lack of recognition shows that it wasn't a council of the entire church in the sense that it transcended its particular era.

A bishop's authority doesn't come from his local church, though as its leader, he remains tied to it and can represent it accordingly.[271] The rediscovery of these connections to the local church from the period of the early Church Fathers was also supposed to be laid out in the examination of the early church's idea of a council and synod. At that time, the bishops tried to bring not only their own theological points of view into the discussion, but they also wanted the concerns of their parish to be heard. However, not all the concerns and objections of a particular local parish could be presented because not all of the church bishops could participate in an ecumenical council. A council—that is, a synod—would then act, based on the trust placed in it, to adequately express the sense of faith of all the faithful so

267. See Hermann Josef Sieben, *Die Konzilsidee der Alten Kirche* (Paderborn, Germany: Ferdinand Schöningh, 1979), 162. It is especially noteworthy that councils have been viewed as political tools for restoring peace to a kingdom ever since Emperor Constantine convened the First Ecumenical Council. Theological concerns were subordinate to this purpose. See Franz Dünzl, *A Brief History of the Doctrine of the Trinity in the Early Church*, trans. John Bowden (London: T&T Clark, 2007), 61–62.
268. Likewise, the primary goal was to restore unity to the empire. Clarifying the theological implications of unity was a secondary goal.
269. See Dünzl, *Brief History*, 79–86.
270. See Sieben, *Konzilsidee*, 362.
271. See Kehl, *Kirche*, 432–35.

that doctrinal resolutions not only represented the views of the episcopate but were resolutions representing the faith of the entirety of the faithful and would therefore find acceptance and recognition.[272] It is neither obvious nor understandable outside a historical context why a council would even have authority and total doctrinal sovereignty. The acknowledgment of this authority only became possible later through the historical development of the concept of a council or a synod and its reception.[273]

Therefore, the authority of the first four ecumenical councils didn't exist from the start but developed over time. This authority depended on their reception throughout the history of the church and doctrine. In part, they should be viewed not as ecumenical councils but rather, from a historical point of view, as regional, specialized synods. The relevance of these first four ecumenical councils was emphasized later by Pope Gregory the Great; he viewed them as analogous to the four gospels.[274]

In accordance with the focus of this analysis, questions of when, where, and by whom a council or a synod was received are not decisive.[275] To be sure, these questions are important, but of much greater importance is whether a council's resolutions continue to be accepted and have thereby been proven to be of lasting validity. In principle, reception is not an act of pure obedience. Rather, faith and revelation share a personal quality: they are both existential events of personal encounter. It is therefore not a question of discerning that particular statements are formally correct. It is rather a matter of understanding and accepting the relevance and validity of these statements to one's own life.[276]

Hans-Georg Gadamer's claim, based on his hermeneutical perspective, that one can't fully grasp doctrinal statements until one has applied them to one's own horizon of living is especially relevant to this discussion.[277] Rahner takes up this theme

272. See Schatz, "Rezeption," 95.
273. See Schatz, 94–95.
274. See Schatz, 104.
275. On this point, one must emphasize the importance of Rome for reception history. See Schatz, "Rezeption": "Rome's most important achievement for the history of councils consists in assuring a clear line of continuity: 'True' councils, that have been recognized by Rome, endure in every case, and in questions of faith, at the very least, are defended against all weaknesses. Councils that contradict these are rejected. This consistency can't be determined for any other institution, for any other patriarch, and above all, not for any imperial rule. Without this clear line from Rome, this continuity would probably never have happened" (107).
276. See Ratzinger, *Problem*, 19.
277. See Gadamer, *Truth and Method*, 328, 404.

when he addresses the claim that there is no significant, underlying difference between an analytic, academic understanding of doctrine and that of a believer: "But in actual fact this is merely apparent. In fact this existential acceptance or refusal opens up or shuts out the whole view of the reality, even though it seems that the profane theoretician of religion can know and say just as much or as little about Christianity as the believing theologian."[278]

Matters that are of relevance to one's own life can only attain a validity that leads the individual to action based on a sense of obligation. According to Gadamer, the validity of a statement for one's own life doesn't happen automatically; a person first recognizes this when they accept and understand it:[279] "Thus acknowledging authority is always connected with the idea that what the authority says is not irrational and arbitrary but can, in principle, be discovered to be true. This is the essence of the authority claimed by the teacher, the superior, the expert."[280]

What is valid in a subjective-personal horizon is no less valid when it is applied to a societal-institutional horizon. There is no authority—as the binding proof of permanent validity—without acceptance.[281] Authority without acceptance is an oxymoron; one can't circumvent the reciprocal structure of granting, practicing, and acknowledging authority.[282] Even though Hermann Josef Pottmeyer recognizes and points out the tension between "reception based on insight" and "reception based on obedience,"[283] he doesn't want to bring them together in an open confrontation; to the contrary, he wants to present a mutual relationship and facilitation of the respective parts to each other.[284] Thus an obligatory teaching of the church can prepare people to recognize their own limiting patterns of thought

278. Rahner, "Dogmatic Statement," 5:50. Just as knowledge is partisan, a perspective opens up a corresponding access to knowledge.
279. Thus reception can be readily understood as existential acceptance through an understanding of its relevance to one's own life. See Pottmeyer, "Rezeption," 75.
280. Gadamer, *Truth and Method*, 281.
281. See Searle, *Making the Social World*, 86–87, 96. It isn't a stretch to take Searle's thinking further and prove a necessary claim of validity based alone on the concept of "doctrine" that already entails, in its semantic development, the horizons of validity and standards via his recognition of collective intentionality that this concept implies. If one wanted a doctrinal stipulation, without a binding high degree of obligation, one would have to come up with a new term. Doctrine implies enduring validity.
282. If authority hasn't been granted or has even been revoked, one is of course dealing no longer with authority but rather with the arbitrary use of power.
283. See Pottmeyer, "Rezeption," 57.
284. See Pottmeyer, 69. In this passage, he states clearly and emphatically that it mustn't come to an excessive demand for obedience by the Ministry of Doctrine because the Ministry of Doctrine would be revoking its own basic principles.

as prejudices and to then put them aside in order to gain deeper insight through a path of (purely temporary) obedience. The ministerial function of doctrine becomes very clear, and one can also understand why it is so necessary within the church.[285] Insights into divine mystery don't lose their validity because those who have insight have already died their worldly death, for these are insights into the eternally valid—that is, God. Therefore, the insights that God, by grace, stipulates through the Holy Spirit are eternally valid and therefore worthy of being handed down to the community of the faithful. Walter Kasper writes about the meaning of tradition in the horizon of temporal development: "It doesn't make sense to play tradition and progress off against each other. Both are mutually dependent on each other. Progress is only possible when a generation stands on the shoulders of the previous one and makes their experiences and achievements their own. Tradition, therefore, has an important function in providing relief. It relieves one from having to go back to the beginning again and again, and from always having to make every experience anew; we thereby become free to make progress."[286]

The *Dogmatic Constitution on the Church* (LG) describes the church as a wandering people in a strange land (LG 6, 851–52; LG 9, 855–56). This shows that the church isn't outside the temporal dimension. To the contrary, it is the contemporary form of the actualization of the kingdom of God and the sacramental manifestation of God's will to salvation (LG 1–2, 849–50; LG 9, 855–56). The church counters the historical and temporal dimension having to do with the *history of salvation* but is nevertheless permanently bound by it because man, as part of creation, is bound by time. The church has a perspective whose goal is outside of time in that the church is making a pilgrimage toward the kingdom of the Father and is being led there under the guidance of the Holy Spirit in order to find there the fulfillment of creation through an encounter with God.[287] However, it is implicit and therefore clear from the following passage that for Kehl, the ecclesiastical community of the faithful mustn't be limited to the current generation:

285. See Pottmeyer, 78–80.
286. Kasper, "Tradition," 381.
287. See Kehl, *Kirche*, 91–92, 152. Kehl places great importance on the goal-oriented perspective of the church because it prevents one from viewing the church as a static institution. Its essence must always be considered in the context of eschatological reservation. See also Kehl, *Eschatologie*, 91–95.

> *Catholicism* can be easily tied to the dimension of the Church that is concerned with the theology of creation and eschatology. Of course, this concept of Catholicism expresses in its literal, original patristic sense . . . the universal breadth of the Church that spans the entire globe. . . . Its theological foundation is based on God's universal will for salvation. The triune God grants his own self-communication to the Church as its "primary recipient," so to speak, with the entire fullness of his love (Eph 1:23; 3:17ff.), in order to proclaim and impart through the Church, as an "instrumental sign" (LG 1, p. 849), his reconciling love for all of creation. Because God is always concerned, first and last, about the salvation of all of creation, which he wants to transform into the kingdom of his peace, his justice, and his life.[288]

The ecclesiastical community spans generations so that even the principle of community, in which an individual can find a place in the "We" of the church, can be viewed, in accordance with the Ignatian *sentire cum ecclesia*, as a cross-generational statement of solidarity.[289] This solidarity, however, shouldn't be a duty of obedience based on an incorrect understanding of fideism; it should have its basis in the hope and the faith that the church in its totality is infallible because God preserves, steers, and leads the church through the Holy Spirit and the truly present presence of Jesus Christ.[290] God bestows the *sensus fidelium* upon the faithful of the church in a grace-filled manner.[291] Because God holds and keeps the faithful in faith and doesn't allow the church to lapse in its faith, the reception of doctrinal documents can be understood in the *longue durée* as an indirect sealing of the theological accuracy of the relevant statements and decisions. Man can't see God's face (Exod 33:20), but he can infer God's impact from God's actions in the world. To be sure, there is a multilayered, indirect statement in this. Nevertheless, this is a statement founded on hope because Jesus promised his community of disciples that the Holy Spirit would always lead them more deeply to the truth (John 16:5–15).

288. Kehl, *Kirche*, 129–30.
289. See Kehl, 19. See also Johanna Rahner, "Häresie," in *Neues Lexikon der katholischen Dogmatik*, ed. Wolfgang Beinert and Bertram Stubenrauch (Freiburg, Germany: Herder, 2012), 305.
290. See Kasper, *Church*, 166, 171–72, 262–65.
291. See Kehl, *Kirche*, 109.

In order to understand the church's reception as pneumatologically influenced, there is good reason to consider it worthy of greater authority. However, this argument—that the reception is pneumatologically conditioned—can also be applied *ex negativo* to the nonreception of doctrinal decisions. Then the nonreception of a doctrinal decision can be viewed from now on as a pneumatological correction through the *sensus fidelium*. God doesn't leave his church alone, but God also doesn't force it into the straitjacket of a *societas perfecta* that is characterized neither by perfectability nor by stasis and immobility. The demand for renewal of the church, as can be found in LG 6 (852) and UR 6 (913),[292] implies neither an ecclesiastical laziness insofar as the Spirit will regulate everything nor a spiritual activism that requires the overly human elements to be cleansed in a radical revision. The synthesis of divine offering and leadership as well as human acceptance, freedom, and cocreativity should serve as a framework for the pilgrimage of God's people to the kingdom of the Father, during which a renewal of the church, and its essence and mission, could happen.

To turn our attention once again to the problem of the history of doctrine, the event of divine self-revelation serves as our starting point. God reveals himself to man within time, and due to the lack of coercion of divine love (1 Cor 13; 1 John 4:8, 16), it becomes man's responsibility to recognize his revealed offering and put it into words. This culminates in the incarnation and God's self-revelation (DV 2, 972): Jesus Christ does not proclaim himself as the content of his own message. The core of Christ's message constitutes the dawning and the coming of the kingdom of God at the end of time; Christ is the sole promulgator of this message (Mark 1:15; Luke 11:20).[293] It therefore required reflection, at a much later time, for Jesus Christ, through the assistance of the Holy Spirit, to be recognized as the content of faith; in this process, Christianity attained this knowledge and was also guided to the understanding that Jesus Christ himself is "the way, and the truth, and the life" (John 14:6).

292. See Bernd Jochen Hilberath, *Theologischer Kommentar zum Dekret über den Ökumenismus. Unitatis redintegratio*, in *HThK*, vol. 3: "The necessary renewal of the Church is called renovatio, but also reformatio. . . . Not based on the wording, but rather on the matter at hand, there is talk of the 'constant reform' (perennis reformatio) that the Church 'continuously needs' (perpetuo indiget), and of the principle of 'ecclesia semper reformanda' that was promoted by the Reformation. The theological justification derives from the pilgrim status of the Church, *insofar* as the Church represents a 'human and earthly institution' (in other words, not *insofar* as the Church represents a divine charitable institution)" (135).

293. See Kasper, *Dogma*, 11, 238–44.

It should be noted here that this constitutes an individual's profession of faith in a public setting in which the individual makes a commitment to this statement; in a manner of speaking, one risks one's own "I."[294] This presents the problem of truth as a dangerous undertaking because one can't rule out the danger of having one's credibility rejected.

An appeal to the truth—that is, making a statement within one's horizon and taking responsibility toward the work involved—does not guarantee the validity of the statement but rather can be viewed as a marker of an attitude that would connect the statement to the individual person.[295] Throughout church history, one can cite multiple examples to demonstrate that a statement of faith in the form of a profession of faith is not an automatic guarantee of orthodoxy. In multiple cases, those who have removed themselves from the ecclesiastical community due to heresies have been required to draw up a profession of faith as a Symbolon, as proof of their own orthodoxy; through its acceptance, they would be rehabilitated by the ecclesiastical community.[296] The heterodox person draws up his own profession of faith, but he doesn't have the authority to recognize his own orthodoxy. The confirmation of orthodoxy is the responsibility of the ecclesiastical community; this community is in a position to differentiate heterodoxy from orthodoxy in the long term, beyond the current generation, through a tradition that spans generations of differentiating apostasy from the *sensus fidelium* that is guided by the Holy Spirit.[297]

294. See Agamben, *Sacrament*, 71.

295. Following Agamben, one sees the potential for perjury in every profession of faith or in every oath; this potentiality can't be structurally excluded but rather opens up the possibility of being able to make subjective statements. See also Agamben, *Sacrament*: "Every naming is, in fact, double: it is a blessing or a curse. A blessing, if the word is full, if there is a correspondence between the signifier and the signified, between words and things: a curse if the word is empty, if there remains, between the semiotic and the semantic, a void and a gap. Oath and perjury, bene-diction and male-diction correspond to this double possibility inscribed in the *logos*, in the experience by means of which the living being has been constituted as speaking being" (69–70).

296. The most prominent case is probably Arius, but going beyond his example, a profession of faith as a Symbolon was an instrument with a shibboleth logic that represented either orthodoxy, and thereby membership in the church community, or heterodoxy and excommunication. See also Dassmann, *Kirchengeschichte*, 2/2:33; and Rufinus, *Commentary*, 542–43. This makes it clear that the provisions for fulfillment of one's own orthodoxy can't be coerced through manipulation.

297. The fact that many faithful were judged to be heterodox and heretical due to political constellations and their own personal profiles, despite (apparent) orthodoxy, unfortunately also shows the human side of the church; the church is often burdened by sin and egoism and has thus been repeatedly prevented from doing justice to its ministerial function as the messenger for and proof of the kingdom of God.

Man attempts to answer the questions, "Who is God?" and "Of what relevance is God to an individual's life and to all of creation?" Proof, as a statement of orthodoxy, is weighed on God's side due to the reception of the pilgrim church; in this way, a statement becomes a communal force that builds identity within the church because God allows it to be acknowledged as orthodoxy via the *sensus fidelium* without glossing over the ontological boundary between human speech and God's word.[298] Such a statement is communicative language but not revelation:

> It is far more important for the believer to be placed in relationship with God's *reality* through the *Word* of the message; in other words, the encounter with God is not the sum of insights. If this is the way things are, revelation can't simply be defined by the number of statements. To the contrary, words only have a communicative function at the completion of the encounter from which they arose and into which they want to return. Words therefore demand their own particular meaning based on each person's use of the words (and the "translation" that comes with it), for this person alone can keep the original meaning in mind.[299]

But human language, due to its formulation out of spiritual faith, retains an internal authority that conditions the pneumatological *intentio operis* but is never conclusively (or unambiguously, persuasively) recognizable. Through the communal reception of the church by the Holy Spirit, professions of faith and doctrinal resolutions maintain an internally rational yet externally effective authority that makes it possible to access the *intentio operis* in its orthodox dimension. An intersection between the *intentio operis* and the *intentio lectoris* arises so that the authority can appropriate the word as its own. The guarantee of an orthodox statement doesn't originate in the speaking subject; it occurs through divine acceptance in its reception and its transmission in tradition.

Everything that man attempts to grasp about God through language is undertaken in the hope that God will have demonstrated its validity. One can't exclude the possibility that a profession of faith may be fallible, based on man's epistemological

298. See Marion, *God*, 140–41; and Ratzinger, *Problem*, 25.
299. Ratzinger, *Problem*, 39.

position, but the fact that it will nevertheless be drawn up and presented to the (ecclesiastical) public is in part motivated by the knowledge that devout speech, as a statement of existential hope, already presumes trust and hope in God and the ecclesiastical community.

Even if it appears, at first glance, paradoxical after this analysis that the magisterium can and does make infallible statements in its ecclesiastical condition, it must be maintained that these statements remain, in regard to their character, theological statements that don't involve, and mustn't entail, any coerced evidence.[300] This would place God on the same level as human knowledge and would take away man's freedom to make the leap of faith. An Absolute God can't be grasped, and thereby limited, by the contingent medium of human speech. Man can only speak about God through analogy, and the church is aware of this (DH, 806).[301] It is therefore valid to maintain this on the level of linguistics and epistemology.

But there is a deeper level of internal rationality and plausibility, beyond the purely profane surface, that is based on the fact that God does not revoke his promises and he himself does not commit perjury: God keeps his word.[302] His commitment to support his apostles and the ecclesiastical community continues to remain valid (John 14:15–31); hence one can even dare to take the next step and assert that the church has structural guidance through the Holy Spirit and therefore, in essence, can't go astray in its church Being (Kirchesein).[303] Henceforth, one can do justice to the infallibility of doctrinal statements because the authority that conditions their infallibility is located not in the church itself but rather in the fact that the church is the location of the mystery of the

300. See Kehl, *Kirche*, 361. These are, and remain, statements of hope "because this never-ceasing *certainty* of faith that is based on God, and that is calm in the face of the constant changes of history, has nothing to do with the often anxiety-laden *certainty* of one's own desire for knowledge and possessions." Kehl, 361.

301. See Ratzinger, *Problem*, 25. Everything that pertains to access to God through language is also valid for access to ecclesiastical identity; just as the church can't define God, it also can't define itself. See Hoff, *Ekklesiologie*: "Just as the Church can't ever express God's mystery other than through the grammar of apophatic theology, the Church also can't express its own reality other than through the mode of a referenced identity" (51).

302. See Agamben, *Sacrament*, 50. According to Agamben, in a strictly literal sense, only God himself can take an oath—in taking an oath, man is *attempting* to imitate God.

303. See Kasper, *Church*, 165–68.

encounter with God and therefore possesses a sacramental character (LG 1, 849; LG 3, 850).[304]

If the church were to present its own statements in a form that indicated only relative validity, the church would fail to recognize its own essence and would, above all, reveal that its own hope is only relative and limited; the church wouldn't trust (in its most existential manner) in God's comforting words and his guidance and leadership through the Holy Spirit (Matt 6:19–34; John 14:15–31; 16:4–15). Plagued by these doubts, the church couldn't proclaim the message of hope of Jesus Christ, "the light of the nations" (LG 1, 849), to the world because it would have too little hope.[305] According to Walter Kasper, one must also keep in mind that doctrinal statements are, first and foremost, statements of living hope toward God. God's truth is a fulfilling hope that may be accepted with confidence: "The truth of this God can only be acknowledged in the mode of trusting hope, but can never be anticipated with a knowing grasp."[306]

304. See Meuffels, Gott:

> The authority of the Catholic Church—its hierarchical bureaucracy is a counterpart to the individual, the local parish, and the world—is founded, according to *Lumen gentium* (LG 1, p. 849; LG 3, p. 850), essentially in the mystery, i.e., the sacramental character of the Church. The Church is therefore historically embedded in the event of God's revelation—as the actual mystery—that is, as a real-symbolic representation of God's Christological-pneumatological act of salvation that affects us in this world. Whereas the loss of a mystery-sacramental understanding of the Church leads to an erroneous assessment of the institutional character of the Church as a whole, conversely, a mystery-sacramental understanding must lead towards Christ through a continuous self-surpassing of the institution of the Church itself. In this regard, the institution is a symbolic expression of God's *predetermined* act of salvation, but, based on its essence, it is simultaneously a realization of the mystery of the love freely given to us by the Creator and Redeemer, and is therefore in its innermost core *dialogically* oriented towards *Communio*. Situated between God and man, the existence of the Church is always grounded in a dual "outside itself." For one thing, the Church exists in a *différance-relationship* towards divine action (*différence*-quality of the relationship) just like the Easter-Pentecost foundation ascribed to it (*possibility of* relationship in the *différence*). The Church is therefore granted its "spiritual power" exclusively through God's actions in relationship to the individual and the world in this arrangement (the Church in its *otherness* in relation to the world). On the other hand, the Church, as the messenger of the *incarnated* Word of God. is nevertheless totally embedded in human structures (the social order of the Church) and media (word and symbol), in order to reach everyone in this way who it represents, through supplicating prayer and liturgy before God (the Church in its Otherness toward God). (244)

305. See Kehl, *Kirche*, 92.
306. Kasper, *Dogma*, 104.

4

Conclusion

Christianity doesn't believe in an impersonal theorem with a dialectical structure or in an anonymous Absolute, an unmoved mover totally detached from the world, that will never be in close proximity to man because it never intersects man's realm. Furthermore, the content of Christian faith wasn't drawn up at a desk in an ivory tower where man, on his own initiative, managed to clear a path toward the Absolute.

The Christian God is the God of history; he is the God of Abraham, Isaac, and Jacob, and he is in close proximity to these men. He protects them and guides them throughout history, and he wants to be in close proximity to them (Exod 3). The inclusion of Pontius Pilate in many professions of faith (DH, 11–36) is not a historical oddity that can be disregarded or pushed aside; it provides a historical anchor point to ensure that Christian faith culminates in the event of the cross and the resurrection and that it is not at risk of becoming another suspicious myth of history. God became part of human history because he became man; he revealed himself without imposing or forcing himself upon man. The invitation to faith was made out of freedom and love. God intrudes directly into human reality and becomes part of it. However, man's encounter with God is very different from the Real in Lacan; it is, admittedly, provocative and irritating, and even God's divinity is characterized by a restlessness. Yet God's intrusion into man's world isn't unsettling, it isn't frightening, and it isn't an experience of horror and dread because God, out of solidarity and in sympathy with man, accepts man's humanness (Menschsein). God fully remains himself and thus reveals not only a part of himself in a mediated form. The form of the communication thereby becomes a part of the message: the Real intrudes into reality in an *irritatingly friendly* manner in the symbolic form of mediation of being human (Menschseins). Through his self-revelation, Jesus Christ is the symbol of the Real for man. Jesus Christ's being human (Menschsein) is not an additional or even accidental part of his message; to the contrary, Christ represents an essential part of revelation.

Man needed time to process and reflect upon this knowledge and also to become open to the Holy Spirit. The superficiality of viewing Jesus Christ only in his humanness (Menschsein) was readily acknowledged, but this transition from the surface (the Symbolic) to the depth (the Real) of this Divine Being couldn't be successful without the hermeneutical support of the Holy Spirit. This made it possible for man to recognize that Jesus Christ's act of salvation is a divine event in which God intrudes directly into human reality. But this knowledge needed a form of expression, and it needed to be communicated because it isn't only tied to the individual subject; rather, as is impressively presented in the Emmaus episode (Luke 24:13–35), it is a recognition by the community of the faithful in a transsubjective manner. Christian faith is the Faith of the church (*fides ecclesiae*); its being encompasses Catholicism in its original meaning. Numerous opinions and perspectives exist as a result of the surplus, supergreatness, and transcendence of God.[1] God grants man the space to develop himself and to verbalize his theological discoveries because God is love, and he doesn't force (1 John 4:8; 1 John 4:16; 1 Cor 13:4–7). The initial gesture of revelation originates from God wherein man is granted not only the freedom but also the means for learning so that he can understand that this revelation is a divine revelation that he can articulate throughout history.

The granting of freedom can unfortunately also lead to its misuse and to the transgression of God-granted boundaries. Instead of trusting the Holy Spirit as the hermeneutic interpreter of divine truth, the heretic asserts that he himself has sovereign power over interpretation; he attempts to reveal the mystery of God through human concepts and to make it understandable to man. The remainder of the Real that doesn't rise to the surface is dragged into the light of human reason, making it impossible to recognize his divinity.

The church is not only on a pilgrimage throughout history toward the kingdom of God, but it also wanders through human knowledge. The church struggles to find the right language to explain the importance that God has for man and the whole of creation through his essence, his plan for salvation, and his influence. In the process, the church, as an ecclesiastical entity (Kirchesein), can't fall short

1. See Pseudo-Dionysius, *The Divine Names*, in *The Complete Works*, trans. Colm Luibheid (New York: Paulist, 1987), 49–50.

because God guides and supports the church without reducing human freedom. The church's theology of hope becomes clear and understandable; humanity is redeemed by the new Adam (Rom 5:12–20) and can confidently drop all everyday fears and doubts about its own existence in order to fully trust God (Matt 6:19–34). Because the founding of the church is God's work, God guides his plan of creation confidently to his destination and completion, to a place where the church has a sacramental structure that can mediate this hopeful encounter between God and man in an experiential way (LG 1, 849). Thus the church's identity is also conditioned from the divine side—God remains faithful (2 Thess 3:3). With this structural safeguard, the church, as a whole, can make infallible statements. The church doesn't lose hope because God guides the church and grants her faith (John 14:26–27). The community of the faithful can't err in the spiritual *sensus fidelium* (LG 12, 858). An ecclesiastical statement is endorsed and sealed in its derived and unerring validity when it has been received, acknowledged, and accepted by the entire community of the faithful that spans generations. However, there is never a moment of time in history when the entire community of the faithful can express communal acceptance, nor a time when all bishops are present and can vote as representatives of their local churches at their highest doctrinal forum—when an ecumenical council has been convened. Therefore, doctrinal proclamations happen through a leap of faith, in anticipation of their acceptance by the entire community of the faithful, in terms of both obedience and understanding because they are reciprocally conditioned. Christian hope is not a force that is limited to the present; it looks to the future and to man's new freedom in the coming of the kingdom of God. Therefore, the church is, as it were, a sacramental place to encounter God; it is a place of anticipation of the completed kingdom of God. The church's statements, in the spiritual *sensus fidelium*, therefore have a proleptic role in the unconcealed encounter between God and man.

The church makes statements by taking a leap of faith and believing that God will have recognized them as true statements via the *sensus fidelium*. Therefore, man doesn't have sovereign power over God in and through language; however, as a person of faith, as a member of the church, he hopes that the Holy Spirit will guide him more deeply into the truth (John 16:5–15). In conclusion, it must therefore be maintained that God does not limit man's freedom despite all the possibilities for error and that within history itself, through the assistance of the Holy Spirit, God has made it possible for man to recognize everything that he approves of and that corresponds to his will. God doesn't give man ready-made sentential knowledge; rather, God's initial move through revelation gives man, as a member of the ecclesiastical community, the spiritual tools for knowledge so that he can appropriately understand and existentially accept its meaning. Everything that is presented to the faithful thereby receives remaining prevalence—that is, infallible validity—by becoming the *depositum fidei* through the *sensus fidelium*. The words of the church have no immediate evidential validity in their (profane) human appearance;[2] however, God can approve these words by granting them a lasting and supratemporal validity through the church's reception by the *sensus fidelium*.

2. On the surface, they remain truly human words. The church itself, analogous to the incarnate mystery, has a truly human and a truly divine nature (LG 8, 854). This analogy can also be applied to the words of the church. The words of the church remain truly human statements: If they are true and infallible statements by the church with everlasting validity, *then* these words also have a truly divine authority.

Selected Bibliography

Unless otherwise indicated, all references to Vatican I and Vatican II cite the following Latin-English edition: *Decrees of the Ecumenical Councils*, vol. 2, *Trent to Vatican II*, ed. Norman P. Tanner (London: Sheed & Ward, 1990). Vatican II references give the abbreviated title of the relevant section, followed by the page number; this avoids potential confusion due to the complexities of the dual numbering system of chapters and paragraphs. Multiple references are separated by a semicolon. The following abbreviations and pagination to individual sections of the text are used:

DV *Dei verbum: Dogmatic Constitution on Divine Revelation*, 971–981

GS *Gaudium et spes: Pastoral Constitution on the Church in the World of Today*, 1069–1135

LG *Lumen gentium: Dogmatic Constitution on the Church*, 849–900

UR *Unitatis redintegratio: Decree on Ecumenism*, 908–920

Other abbreviations used in this work are the following:

AL *Augustinus-Lexikon*, ed. Cornelius Mayer, vols. 1–3 (Basel, Switzerland: Schwabe, 1984–2010)

CCC *Catechism of the Catholic Church* (Washington, DC: United States Catholic Conference, 1994)

DH Heinrich Denzinger, *Enchiridion symbolorum definitionum et declarationum de rebus fidei et morum / Compendium of Creeds, Definitions, and Declarations on Matters of Faith and Morals, Latin-English*, ed. Peter Hünermann, 43rd ed., revised, enlarged, and in collaboration with Helmut Hoping, ed. Robert Fastiggi and Anne Englund Nash for the English edition (San Francisco: Ignatius, 2012)

GdK Michael Schmaus, *Der Glaube der Kirche*, vols. 1–6 (St. Ottilien, Germany: EOS Verlag, 1979–1982)

HThK *Herders theologischer Kommentar zum Zweiten Vatikanischen Konzil*, ed. Peter Hünermann and Bernd Jochen Hilberath, vols. 1–5 (Freiburg, Germany: Herder, 2009)

LThK *Lexikon für Theologie und Kirche*, ed. Walter Kasper et al., vols. 1–11 (Freiburg, Germany: Herder, 2006)

MThZ *Münchener Theologische Zeitschrift*

Agamben, Giorgio. *Homo Sacer: Sovereign Power and Bare Life*. Translated by Daniel Heller-Roazen. Stanford, CA: Stanford University Press, 1998.

——. *The Sacrament of Language: An Archaeology of the Oath*. Translated by Adam Kotsko. Stanford, CA: Stanford University Press, 2011.

——. *The Time That Remains: A Commentary on the Letter to the Romans*. Translated by Patricia Dailey. Stanford, CA: Stanford University Press, 2005.

Andia, Ysabel de. *Homo vivens: Incorruptibilité et divinisation de l'homme selon Irénée de Lyon*. Paris: Études Augustiniennes, 1986.

Anselm of Canterbury. *Proslogion*. Translated by M. J. Charlesworth. Notre Dame, IN: University of Notre Dame Press, 1979.

Aristotle. *Metaphysics*. In *The Complete Works of Aristotle: The Revised Oxford Translation*, edited by Jonathan Barnes, 2:1552–1728. Princeton, NJ: Princeton University Press, 1984.

——. *Politics*. In *The Complete Works of Aristotle: The Revised Oxford Translation*, edited by Jonathan Barnes, 2:1986–2129. Princeton, NJ: Princeton University Press, 1984.

Augustine. *The City of God against the Pagans*. Edited and translated by R. W. Dyson. Cambridge Texts in the History of Political Thought. Cambridge: Cambridge University Press, 1998.

——. *The Confessions*. Vol. 1/1 of *The Works of Saint Augustine: A Translation for the 21st Century*, edited by John E. Rotelle, translated by Maria Boulding. Hyde Park, NY: New City Press, 2015.

——. *Homilies on the Gospel of John 1–40*. Vol. 1/12 of *The Works of Saint Augustine: A Translation for the 21st Century*, edited by Allan D. Fitzgerald, translated by Edmund Hill. Hyde Park, NY: New City Press, 2009.

——. "Letter #120." In *Letters 100–155 (Epistulae)*, edited by Boniface Ramsey, translated by Roland Teske, 129–140. Vol. 2/2 of *The Works of Saint Augustine: A Translation for the 21st Century*. Hyde Park, NY: New City Press, 2003.

——. "A Treatise on the Gift of Perseverance." In *Nicene and Post-Nicene Fathers*, 1st ser. Vol. 5, edited by Philip Schaff, translated by Peter Holmes, Robert Ernest Wallis, and Benjamin Warfield, 525–552. Peabody, MA: Hendrickson, 1994.

——. "A Treatise on the Spirit and the Letter." In *Nicene and Post-Nicene Fathers*, 1st ser. Vol. 5, edited by Philip Schaff, translated by Peter Holmes, Robert Ernest Wallis, and Benjamin Warfield, 80–114. Peabody, MA: Hendrickson, 1994.

——. *The Trinity / De Trinitate*. Vol. 1/5 of *The Works of Saint Augustine: A Translation for the 21st Century*, edited by John E. Rotelle, translated by Edmund Hill. Hyde Park, NY: New City Press, 2015.

Austin, John Langshaw. *How to Do Things with Words: The William James Lectures Delivered at Harvard University in* 1955. Cambridge, MA: Harvard University Press, 1962.

Bacht, Heinrich. "Die Rolle des orientalischen Mönchtums in den kirchenpolitischen Auseinandersetzungen um Chalkedon, 431–519." In *Das Konzil von Chalkedon: Geschichte und Gegenwart*. Vol. 2, *Entscheidung um Chalkedon*, edited by Aloys Grillmeier and Heinrich Bacht, 193–314. Würzburg, Germany: Echter Verlag, 1953.

Badiou, Alain. *Being and Event*. Translated by Oliver Feltham. London: Continuum, 2006.

——. *Ethics: An Essay on the Understanding of Evil*. Translated by Peter Hallward. London: Verso, 2001.

——. *Saint Paul: The Foundation of Universalism*. Translated by Ray Brassier. Stanford, CA: Stanford University Press, 2003.

Barthes, Roland. "The Death of the Author." In *Image, Music, Text*, translated by Stephen Heath, 142–148. New York: Hill and Wang, 1977.

Becker, Jürgen. *Jesus of Nazareth*. Translated by James E. Crouch. New York: Walter de Gruyter, 1998.

Böhm, Thomas. *Die Christologie des Arius: Dogmengeschichtliche Überlieferung unter besonderer Berücksichtigung der Hellenisierungsfrage*. Studien zur Theologie und Geschichte 7. St. Ottilien, Germany: EOS Verlag, 1991.

——. "Glaube und Inkulturation: Gab es einen 'Zwang' zur Heterodoxie in der Spätantike?" In *Glaube und Kultur: Begegnung zweier Welten?*, edited by Thomas Böhm in collaboration with Benedikt Barth, 109–139. Freiburg, Germany: Herder, 2009.

Bovon, François. *Luke 3: A Commentary on the Gospel of Luke, 19:28–24:53*. Edited by Helmut Koester. Translated by James Crouch. Minneapolis: Fortress, 2012.

Bründl, Jürgen. *Gottes Nähe: Der Heilige Geist und das Problem der Negativität in der Theologie*. Freiburg, Germany: Herder, 2010.

Buber, Martin. "Autobiographical Fragments." In *The Philosophy of Martin Buber*, edited by Paul Arthus Schilp and Maurice Friedman, 3–37. La Salle, IL: Open Court, 1967.

Bürkle, Horst. "Mythos, Mythologie, 1. Begriff., II. Religionsgeschichtlich." In *LThK*. Vol. 7, cols. 597–600.

Dalferth, Ingolf U. "Religion und Wahrheit." In *Wahrheit in Perspektiven: Probleme einer offenen Konstellation*, edited by Ingolf U. Dalferth and Philipp Stoellger, 195–232. Religion in Philosophy and Theology 14. Tübingen, Germany: Mohr Siebeck, 2004.

Dalferth, Ingolf U., and Philipp Stoellger. "Perspektive und Wahrheit: Einleitende Hinweise auf eine klärungsbedürftige Problemgeschichte." In *Wahrheit in Perspektiven: Probleme einer offenen Konstellation*, edited by Ingolf U. Dalferth and Philipp Stoellger, 1–28, Religion in Philosophy and Theology 14. Tübingen, Germany: Mohr Siebeck, 2004.

Dallmayr, Horst. *Die grossen vier Konzilien: Nicaea, Konstantinopel, Ephesus, Chalcedon*. Munich, Germany: Kösel-Verlag, 1961.

Dassmann, Ernst. *Kirchengeschichte 2/2: Theologie und innerkirchliches Leben bis zum Ausgang der Spätantike*. Kohlhammer Studienbücher Theologie 11/2. Stuttgart, Germany: Kohlhammer, 1999.

Dawkins, Richard. *The God Delusion*. Boston: Houghton Mifflin, 2006.

Derrida, Jacques. "Différance." In *Margins of Philosophy*, translated by Alan Bass, 1–27. Chicago: University of Chicago Press, 1982.

——. *On the Name*. Edited by Thomas Dutoit. Translated by David Wood, John P. Leavey Jr., and Ian McLeod. Stanford, CA: Stanford University Press, 1995.

——. *Writing and Difference*. Translated by Alan Bass. Chicago: University of Chicago Press, 1978.

Dohmen, Christoph. "Paradies. II. Biblisch-theologisch." In *LThK*. Vol. 7, cols. 1360–1362.

Drecoll, Volker Henning. "Gratia." In AL. Vol. 3, cols. 182–242.

Dünzl, Franz. *A Brief History of the Doctrine of the Trinity in the Early Church*. Translated by John Bowden. London: T&T Clark, 2007.

Ebeling, Gerhard. *Dogmatik des christlichen Glaubens*. Vol. 1, *Prolegomena. Erster Teil. Der Glaube an Gott, den Schöpfer der Welt*. Tübingen, Germany: Mohr Siebeck, 1979.

Ebner, Martin. "A. 1. Der christliche Kanon." In *Einleitung in das Neue Testament*, edited by Martin Ebner and Stefan Schreiber, 9–52. Kohlhammer Studienbücher Theologie 6. Stuttgart, Germany: Kohlhammer, 2008.

——. "B. III. Evangelium." In *Einleitung in das Neue Testament*, edited by Martin Ebner and Stefan Schreiber, 112–124. Kohlhammer Studienbücher Theologie 6. Stuttgart, Germany: Kohlhammer, 2008.

——. "B. V. Das Markusevangelium." In *Einleitung in das Neue Testament*, edited by Martin Ebner and Stefan Schreiber, 154–183. Kohlhammer Studienbücher Theologie 6. Stuttgart, Germany: Kohlhammer, 2008.

Eco, Umberto. "Between Author and Text." In *Interpretation and Overinterpretation*, edited by Stefan Collini and with contributions by Richard Rorty, Jonathan Culler, and Christine Brooke-Rose, 67–88. Cambridge: Cambridge University Press, 1992.

——. *The Limits of Interpretation*. Bloomington: Indiana University Press, 1990.

Egger, Wilhelm. *Galater Brief, Philipperbrief, Philemonbrief*. Die Neue Echter Bibel: Kommentar zum Neuen Testament mit der Einheitsübersetzung 9, 11, 15. Würzburg, Germany: Echter Verlag, 1988.

Engelmann, Peter. "Einführung: Postmoderne und Dekonstruktion; Zwei Stichwörter zur zeitgenössischen Philosophie." In *Postmoderne und Dekonstruktion: Texte französischer Philosophen der Gegenwart*, edited by Peter Engelmann, 5–32. Stuttgart, Germany: Reclam, 2007.

Ernst, Stephan. *Grundfragen theologischer Ethik: Eine Einführung*. Munich, Germany: Kösel, 2009.

Eusebius. *The Church History of Eusebius*. In *Nicene and Post-Nicene Fathers*, 2nd ser. Vol. 1, edited by Philip Schaff and Henry Wace, translated by C. A. Heurtley, 73–404. Peabody, MA: Hendrickson, 1994.

Evans, Dylan. *An Introductory Dictionary of Lacanian Psychoanalysis*. London: Routledge, 1996.

Feiner, Johannes. "Offenbarung und Kirche—Kirche und Offenbarung." In *Mysterium Salutis: Grundriss heilsgeschichtlicher Dogmatik*. Vol. 1, *Die Grundlagen heilsgeschichtlicher Dogmatik*, edited by Johannes Feiner and Magnus Löhrer, 497–544. Einsiedeln, Switzerland: Benziger Verlag, 1965.

Finkelde, Dominik. *Politische Eschatologie nach Paulus: Badiou—Agamben—Žižek—Santner*. Vienna: Turia + Kant, 2007.

Fischer, Georg, and Dominik Markl. *Das Buch Exodus*. Neuer Stuttgarter Kommentar: Altes Testament 2. Stuttgart, Germany: Katholisches Bibelwerk, 2009.

Fleteren, Frederick van. "Illuminatio." In AL. Vol. 3, cols. 495–504.

Foucault, Michel. *Discipline and Punish: The Birth of the Prison*. Translated by Alan Sheridan. New York: Vintage, 1979.

Gadamer, Hans-Georg. *Truth and Method*. Translated by Joel Weinsheimer and Donald G. Marshall. 2nd ed. London: Continuum, 2006.

Greshake, Gisbert. *Maria-Ecclesia: Perspektiven einer marianisch grundierten Theologie und Kirchenpraxis*. Regensburg, Germany: F. Pustet, 2014.

——. "Visio beatifica." In *LThK*. Vol. 10, col. 810.

Grillmeier, Aloys. "Die theologische und sprachliche Vorbereitung der christologischen Formel von Chalkedon." In *Das Konzil von Chalkedon: Geschichte und Gegenwart*. Vol. 1, *Der Glaube von Chalkedon*, edited by Aloys Grillmeier and Heinrich Bacht, 5–202. Würzburg, Germany: Echter Verlag, 1951.

Grünwaldt, Klaus. *Gott und sein Volk: Die Theologie der Bibel*. Darmstadt, Germany: Wissenschaftliche Buchgesellschaft, 2006.

Heidegger, Martin. *Being and Time*. Translated by Joan Stambaugh. Revised by Dennis J. Schmidt. Albany: State University of New York Press, 2010.

——. "On the Essence of Truth." In *Basic Writings*, edited by David Farrell Krell, 115–138. New York: HarperCollins, 2008.

——. "The Origin of the Work of Art." In *Basic Writings*, edited by David Farrell Krell, 143–212. New York: HarperCollins, 2008.

Hilberath, Bernd Jochen. "F. Gnadenlehre." In *Handbuch der Dogmatik*. Vol. 2, edited by Theodor Schneider, 3–46. Düsseldorf, Germany: Patmos Verlag, 2000.

——. *Theologischer Kommentar zum Dekret über den Ökumenismus. Unitatis redintegratio*. In HThK. Vol. 3, 69–223.

Hoff, Gregor Maria. *Ekklesiologie*. Gegenwärtig Glauben Denken—Systematische Theologie 6. Paderborn, Germany: Ferdinand Schöningh, 2011.

Höffe, Otfried. *Aristotle*. Translated by Christine Salazer. Albany: State University of New York Press, 2003.

Hoffmann, Paul. "Menschensohn. II. Neues Testament." In *LThK*. Vol. 7, cols. 131–132.

Hoping, Helmut. "Theologischer Kommentar zur Dogmatischen Konstitution über die göttliche Offenbarung, *Dei verbum*." In HThK. Vol. 3, 695–831.

Janowski, Bernd. *Gottes Gegenwart in Israel*. Beiträge zur Theologie des Alten Testaments 1. Neukirchen-Vluyn, Germany: Neukirchener Verlag, 1993.

Jeßing, Benedikt, and Ralph Köhnen. *Einführung in die Neuere deutsche Literaturwissenschaft*. Stuttgart, Germany: J. B. Metzler, 2007.

Kaiser, Otto. *Der Gott des Alten Testaments: Wesen und Wirken; Theologie des Alten Testaments, Teil 2: Jahwe, der Gott Israels, Schöpfer der Welt und des Menschen*. Uni-Taschenbücher 2024. Göttingen, Germany: Vandenhoeck & Ruprecht, 1998.

Kasper, Walter. *The Catholic Church: Nature, Reality and Mission*. Edited by R. David Nelson. Translated by Thomas Hoebel. London: Bloomsbury, 2015.

——. *Dogma unter dem Wort Gottes*. Mainz, Germany: Matthias-Grünewald-Verlag, 1965.

——. "Tradition als theologisches Erkenntnisprinzip." In *Dogmengeschichte und katholische Theologie*, edited by Werner Löser, Karl Lehmann, and Matthias Lutz-Bachmann, 376–403. Würzburg, Germany: Echter Verlag, 1985.

Kehl, Medard. *Die Kirche: Eine katholische Ekklesiologie*. Dettelbach, Germany: Röll, 2009.

——. *Eschatologie*. Würzburg, Germany: Echter Verlag, 1986.

Kierkegaard, Søren. *Fear and Trembling/Repetition*. Edited and translated by Howard V. Hong and Edna H. Hong. Princeton, NJ: Princeton University Press, 1983.

——. *The Sickness unto Death: A Christian Exposition for Upbuilding and Awakening*. Edited and translated by Howard V. Hong and Edna H. Hong. Princeton, NJ: Princeton University Press, 1980.

Klauck, Hans-Josef. *1. Korintherbrief*. Die Neue Echter Bibel: Kommentar zum Neuen Testament mit der Einheitsübersetzung 7. Würzburg, Germany: Echter Verlag, 1987.

Klug, Florian. *Die causa sui im Verhältnis zum unbewegten Beweger: Untersuchungen zum Einfluss der Philosophie des Aristoteles zur Gotteslehre und Schöpfungstheologie Herman Schells*. Pontes 57. Münster, Germany: Lit, 2013.

Körtner, Ulrich H. J. *Einführung in die theologische Hermeneutik*. Einführung Theologie. Darmstadt, Germany: Wissenschaftliche Buchgesellschaft, 2006.

Koster, Mannes Dominikus. "Von der Findung der theologischen Grundsätze." In *Einsicht und Glaube*, edited by Joseph Ratzinger and Heinrich Fries, 280–298. Freiburg, Germany: Herder, 1962.

Köster, Peter. "Gott." In *Nietzsche-Handbuch: Leben—Werk—Wirkung*, edited by Henning Ottmann, 245–248. Stuttgart, Germany: J. B. Metzler, 2011.

Kremer, Jakob. *Lukasevangelium*. Die Neue Echter Bibel: Kommentar zum Neuen Testament mit der Einheitsübersetzung 3. Würzburg, Germany: Echter Verlag, 1988.

Lacan, Jacques. *Die Objektbeziehung, Das Seminar Buch IV* (1956–57). Edited by Jacques-Alain Miller. Translated (from French) by Hans-Dieter Gondek. Vienna: Turia + Kant, 2003.

——. *Écrits: The First Complete Edition in English*. Translated by Bruce Fink, in collaboration with Héloïse Fink and Russell Grigg. New York: W. W. Norton, 2006.

——. *Encore: The Seminar of Jacques Lacan*. Bk. 20, 1972–1973: *On Feminine Sexuality: The Limits of Love and Knowledge*, edited by Jacques-Alain Miller, translated by Bruce Fink. New York: W. W. Norton, 1999.

——. *The Four Fundamental Concepts of Psychoanalysis: The Seminar of Jacques Lacan*. Bk. 11, edited by Jacques-Alain Miller, translated by Alan Sheridan. New York: W. W. Norton, 1998.

——. *On the Names-of-the-Father*. Translated by Bruce Fink. Malden, MA: Polity, 2013.

——. *The Psychoses: The Seminar of Jacques Lacan*. Bk. 3, 1955–1956, edited by Jacques-Alain Miller, translated by Russell Grigg. New York: W. W. Norton, 1993.

Lies, Lothar. "Fides qua—fides quae creditur." In *LThK*. Vol. 3, cols. 1274–1275.

Liessmann, Konrad Paul. *Schönheit*. Vienna: Facultas.wuv, 2009.

——. *Sören Kierkegaard zur Einführung*. Hamburg, Germany: Junius, 2006.

Luz, Ulrich. *Matthew 1–7: A Commentary*. Translated by Wilhelm C. Linss. Minneapolis: Augsburg Fortress, 1989.

Marion, Jean-Luc. *God without Being: Hors-Texte*. Translated by Thomas A. Carlson, with a foreword by David Tracy. Chicago: University of Chicago Press, 2012.

Menke, Karl-Heinz. "Realsymbol." In *LThK*. Vol. 8, cols. 867–868.

Merklein, Helmut. *Der erste Brief an die Korinther: 1, Kapitel 1–4*. Ökumenischer Taschenbuchkommentar zum Neuen Testament 7/1. Gütersloh, Germany: Gütersloher Mohn, 1992.

Meuffels, Otmar. "Der Mut, die Wahrheit beim Namen zu nennen: Gedanken zur Dogmatik." *MThZ* 64, no. 3 (2013): 252–286.

——. *Gott Erfahren: Theologisch-philosophische Bausteine zur Gotteslehre*. Religion in Philosophy and Theology 19. Tübingen, Germany: Mohr Siebeck, 2006.

Müller, Gerhard Ludwig. *Katholische Dogmatik: Für Studium und Praxis der Theologie*. Freiburg, Germany: Herder, 1995.

Nietzsche, Friedrich. *Nachgelassene Fragmente: 1887–1889*. Vol. 13 of *Sämtliche Werke: Kritische Studienausgabe in 15 Bänden*, edited by Giorgio Colli and Mazzino Montinari. Munich, Germany: Deutscher Taschenbuch Verlag / de Gruyter, 1999.

——. "On Truth and Lie in an Extra-Moral Sense." In *The Portable Nietzsche*, translated by Walter Kaufmann, 42–47. New York: Viking, 1954.

——. *The Will to Power*. Edited by Walter Kaufmann. Translated by Walter Kaufmann and R. J. Hollingdale. New York: Random House, 1967.

Novatian. *Treatise concerning the Trinity*. In *Ante-Nicene Fathers*. Vol. 5, edited by Alexander Roberts and James Donaldson, translated by Robert Ernest Wallis, 605–644. Peabody, MA: Hendrickson, 1994.

Pfammater, Josef. *Epheserbrief: Kolosserbrief*. Die Neue Echter-Bibel: Kommentar zum neuen Testament mit der Einheitsübersetzung 10, 12. Würzburg, Germany: Echter Verlag, 1987.

Plato. *Cratylus*. In *The Collected Dialogues of Plato*, edited by Edith Hamilton and Huntington Cairns. Princeton, NJ: Princeton University Press, 1987.

Pottmeyer, Hermann Josef. "Rezeption und Gehorsam—Aktuelle Aspekte einer wiederentdeckten Realität 'Rezeption.'" In *Glaube als Zustimmung: Zur Interpretation kirchlicher Rezeptionsvorgänge*, edited by Wolfgang Beinert, 51–92. Quaestiones disputatae 131. Freiburg, Germany: Herder, 1991.

Pseudo-Dionysius. *The Divine Names*. In *The Complete Works*, translated by Colm Luibheid, 47–131. New York: Paulist, 1987.

Rahner, Johanna. "Häresie." In *Neues Lexikon der katholischen Dogmatik*, edited by Wolfgang Beinert and Bertram Stubenrauch, 305–307. Freiburg, Germany: Herder, 2012.

——. "Lehramt und Glaubenssinn: Anmerkungen zu einem zunehmend schwieriger werdenden dogmatischen Lehrstück." In *Glaube in Gemeinschaft: Autorität und Rezeption in der Kirche*, edited by Markus Knapp and Thomas Söding, 165–181. Freiburg, Germany: Herder, 2014.

Rahner, Karl. "The Theology of the Symbol." In *Theological Investigations*. Vol. 4, *More Recent Writings*, translated by Kevin Smyth, 221–252. Baltimore: Helicon, 1966.

——. "What Is a Dogmatic Statement?" In *Theological Investigations*. Vol. 5, *Later Writings*, translated by Karl-H. Kruger, 42–66. Baltimore: Helicon, 1966.

Rahner, Karl, and Herbert Vorgrimler. *Kleines Konzilskompendium: Sämtliche Texte des Zweiten Vatikanums*. Freiburg, Germany: Herder, 1980.

Ratzinger, Joseph. *Das neue Volk Gottes: Entwürfe zur Ekklesiologie*. Düsseldorf, Germany: Patmos Verlag, 1970.

——. *Das Problem der Dogmengeschichte in der Sicht der katholischen Theologie*. Arbeitsgemeinschaft des Landes Nordrhein-Westfalen, Geisteswissenschaften 139. Cologne: Westdeutscher Verlag, 1966.

Ritter, Adolf Martin. "Dogma und Lehre in der Alten Kirche." In *Handbuch der Dogmen- und Theologiegeschichte*. Vol. 1, *Die Lehrentwicklung im Rahmen der Katholizität*, edited by Carl Andresen, 99–283. Göttingen, Germany: Vandenhoeck & Ruprecht, 1982.

Rufinus. *A Commentary on the Apostles' Creed*. In *Nicene and Post-Nicene Fathers*, 2nd ser. Vol. 3, edited by Philip Schaff and Henry Wace, translated by William Henry Fremantle, 541–563. Peabody, MA: Hendrickson, 1994.

Sander, Hans-Joachim. "Theologischer Kommentar zur Pastoralkonstitution über die Kirche in der Welt von heute, *Gaudium et spes*." In *HThK*. Vol. 4, 581–886.

Sandkühler, Hans Jörg, ed. "Analogie." In *Enzyklopädie Philosophie*. Vol. 1, A–N, 47–52. Hamburg, Germany: Meiner, 1999.

Sattler, Dorothea, and Theodor Schneider. "C. Schöpfungslehre." In *Handbuch der Dogmatik*. Vol. 1, edited by Theodor Schneider, 120–238. Düsseldorf, Germany: Patmos Verlag, 2000.

Saussure, Ferdinand de. *Course in General Linguistics*. Edited by Charles Bally and Albert Sechehaye. Translated by Roy Harris. Chicago: Open Court, 2003.

Schatz, Klaus. "Rezeption ökumenischer Konzilien im ersten Jahrtausend: Schwierigkeiten, Formen der Bewältigung und verweigerte Rezeption." In *Glaube als Zustimmung: Zur Interpretation kirchlicher Rezeptionsvorgänge*, edited by Wolfgang Beinert, 93–122. Quaestiones disputatae 131. Freiburg, Germany: Herder, 1991.

Scheffezyk, Leo. "Paradies. III. Systematisch-theologisch." In *LThK*. Vol. 7, col. 1362.

Schilson, Arno. "Lex orandi—lex credendi." In *LThK*. Vol. 6, cols. 871–872.

Schnackenburg, Rudolf. *The Gospel according to St. John*. Vol. 3, *Commentary on Chapters 13–21*, translated by David Smith and G. A. Kon. New York: Crossroad, 1982.

Schönrich, Gerhard. "Semiotik." In *Enzyklopädie Philosophie*. Vol. 2, O–Z, 1460–1465. Hamburg, Germany: Meiner, 1999.

Schreiber, Stefan. "Briefliteratur im Neuen Testament." In *Einleitung in das Neue Testament*, edited by Martin Ebner and Stefan Schreiber, 250–264. Kohlhammer Studienbücher Theologie 6. Stuttgart, Germany: Kohlhammer, 2008.

Schreiner, Josef. *Theologie des Alten Testaments*. Ergänzungsbände zum Alten Testament 1. Würzburg, Germany: Echter Verlag, 1995.

Searle, John R. *Making the Social World: The Structure of Human Civilization*. Oxford: Oxford University Press, 2010.

Seebass, Horst. *Genesis I: Urgeschichte* (1.1–11.26). Neukirchen-Vluyn, Germany: Neukirchener Verlag, 1996.

——. *Genesis II: Vätergeschichten II* (23.1–36.43). Neukirchen-Vluyn, Germany: Neukirchener Verlag, 1999.

Sieben, Hermann Josef. *Die Konzilsidee der Alten Kirche*. Konziliengeschichte, series B: Untersuchungen. Paderborn, Germany: Ferdinand Schöningh, 1979.

Söll, Georg. *Dogma und Dogmenentwicklung*. Vol. 1/5 of *Das Dasein im Glauben*. Handbuch der Dogmengeschichte. Freiburg, Germany: Herder, 1971.

Straub, Jürgen. *Handlung, Interpretation, Kritik: Grundzüge einer textwissenschaftlichen Handlungs- und Kulturpsychologie*. Perspektiven der Humanwissenschaften 18. Berlin: De Gruyter, 1999.

Striet, Magnus. *In der Gottesschleife: Von religiöser Sehnsucht in der Moderne*. Freiburg, Germany: Herder, 2014.

Tertullian. *The Prescription against Heretics*. In *Ante-Nicene Fathers*. Vol. 3, edited by Alexander Roberts and James Donaldson, translated by Peter Holmes, 243–267. Peabody, MA: Hendrickson, 1994.

TeSelle, Eugene. “Fides.” In AL. Vol. 2, cols. 1333–1340.

Urbina, Ignacio Oritz de. “Das Glaubenssymbol von Chalkedon—sein Text, sein Werden, seine dogmatische Bedeutung.” In *Das Konzil von Chalkedon: Geschichte und Gegenwart*. Vol. 1, *Der Glaube von Chalkedon*, edited by Aloys Grillmeier and Heinrich Bacht, 389–418. Würzburg, Germany: Echter Verlag, 1951.

Utzschneider, Helmut, and Wolfgang Oswald. Exodus 1–15: *International Exegetical Commentary on the Old Testament* (IEKAT), translated by Philip Sumpter. Stuttgart, Germany: Kohlhammer, 2015.

Verweyen, Hansjürgen. *Botschaft eines Toten? Den Glauben Rational Verantworten*. Regensburg, Germany: F. Pustet, 1997.

Vincent of Lérins. *The Commonitory of Vincent of Lérins, for the Antiquity and Universality of the Catholic Faith against the Profane Novelties of All Heresies*. In *Nicene and Post-Nicene Fathers*, 2nd ser. Vol. 11, edited by Philip Schaff and Henry Wace, translated by C. A. Heurtley, 123–159. Peabody, MA: Hendrickson, 1994.

Voderholzer, Rudolf. *Offenbarung, Tradition und Schriftauslegung: Bausteine zu einer christlichen Bibelhermeneutik*. Regensburg, Germany: F. Pustet, 2013.

Weimar, Peter. "Herrlichkeit Gottes. 1. Altes Testament, II. Frühjudentum." In *LThK*. Vol. 5, cols. 21–23.

Wendel, Saskia. "'Nichtsprechendes Sprechen' über Transzendenz: Lyotard—Derrida—Levinas." In *Wie lässt sich über Gott sprechen? Von der negativen Theologie Plotins bis zum religiösen Sprachspiel Wittgensteins*, edited by Werner Schüssler, 271–284. Darmstadt, Germany: Wissenschaftliche Buchgesellschaft, 2008.

Werbick, Jürgen. "Die Autorität der Zeugen—und andere Glaubwürdigkeiten: Ein ekklesiologischer Diskurs über die Glaubwürdigkeit." In *Glaube in Gemeinschaft: Autorität und Rezeption in der Kirche*, edited by Markus Knapp and Thomas Söding, 19–36. Freiburg, Germany: Herder, 2014.

Wilckens, Ulrich. *Der Brief an die Römer, Teilband 2, Römer 6–11*. Evangelisch-katholischer Kommentar zum Neuen Testament (EKK) 6/2. Neukirchen-Vluyn, Germany: Neukirchener Verlag, 1987.

Williams, Rowan. *Arius: Heresy and Tradition*. Rev. ed. Grand Rapids, MI: William B. Eerdmans, 2002.

Winger, Wolfram. "Hubris." In *LThK*. Vol. 5, cols. 350–351.

Wittgenstein, Ludwig. *Tractatus Logico-Philosophicus*. Translated by D. F. Pears and B. F. McGuiness, with an introduction by Bertrand Russell. London: Routledge, 1981.

Zittel, Claus. "Erkenntnis." In *Nietzsche-Handbuch: Leben—Werk—Wirkung*, edited by Henning Ottmann, 219–220. Stuttgart, Germany: J. B. Metzler, 2011.

Žižek, Slavoj. *Event: A Philosophical Journey through a Concept*. Brooklyn: Melvin House, 2014.

——. *The Fragile Absolute: Or, Why Is the Christian Legacy Worth Fighting For?* London: Verso, 2001.

——. *How to Read Lacan*. New York: W. W. Norton, 2006.

——. *Less Than Nothing: Hegel and the Shadow of Dialectical Materialism*. London: Verso, 2012.

——. *On Belief*. New York: Routledge, 2001.

——. *The Ticklish Subject: The Absent Centre of Political Ontology*. London: Verso, 2000.

Zmijewski, Josef. "Hirt. II. Neues Testament." In *LThK*. Vol. 5, cols. 155–157.